Susan Au
is a freelance writer and historian of dance.
She was senior researcher for *Choreography by George
Balanchine: A Catalogue of Works* (revised edition, 1984) and is
a contributor to the *International Encyclopedia of Dance* and the
New Grove Dictionary of Music in the United States; she has
also published numerous articles.

Selma Jeanne Cohen
is the doyenne of American dance historians.
She has published several books and many articles as well as
editing the journal *Dance Perspectives* for seventeen
years. She is editor-in-chief of the
International Encyclopedia of Dance.

D0166704

WORLD OF ART

This famous series
provides the widest available
range of illustrated books on art in all its aspects.
If you would like to receive a complete list
of titles in print please write to:
THAMES AND HUDSON
30 Bloomsbury Street, London WC1B 3QP
In the United States please write to:
THAMES AND HUDSON INC.
500 Fifth Avenue, New York, New York 10110

SUSAN AU

ballet & modern dance

Introduction by Selma Jeanne Cohen

With 137 illustrations, 20 in color

THAMES AND HUDSON

Frontispiece
1 *Martha Graham in* Clytemnestra, 1958.

First published in the United States in 1988
by Thames and Hudson Inc., 500 Fifth Avenue,
New York, New York 10110

Library of Congress Catalog Card Number
87-50193

Printed and bound in Singapore
by C.S. Graphics Pte Ltd.

Contents

Introduction

Susan Au begins this book by remarking that a 20th-century observer would probably have trouble recognizing a 16th-century court ballet as a ballet. So much has changed since then – our ideas about the function of a dance work, about its most suitable venue, the kinds of sound accompaniment and decorations appropriate to it, the skills expected of its performers, the role to be played by the audience with respect to the occasion. What has changed and the manner in which it has changed are detailed in the following pages, that trace the evolution of theatrical dance from a spectacle designed to impress an invited audience with the wealth, taste, and righteousness of their hosts, to a myriad of manifestations designed sometimes to please the eye, sometimes to move the heart, sometimes to alter the moral or political views of spectators from many walks of life who have paid for their tickets of admission.

The history that Ms Au delineates is rich in diversity, diversity that seems just now to be multiplying rapidly. While early developments occupied decades, even centuries, the current scene appears to offer almost annual accruals of innovative productions. Indeed, many a 20th-century observer has had trouble recognizing a 20th-century ballet as a ballet. The puzzlement accelerated in the 1960s when the identity problem expanded to include dance itself. It was difficult enough when the choreographer eliminated entrechats and pirouettes, but when he began to eliminate movement . . . We value the new, but it has given us problems.

This book arrives at an opportune moment. Inundated with dance experiments, seeking to separate the genuine advance from the merely exhibitionist, we have arrived at a time when we need to explore the background of the current 'dance explosion'. Viewing it in isolation from what has gone before, we cannot achieve a balanced perspective. As we read here, we see how the present was formed through extension, revision and revolt out of the past. That dance is changing is not new; only the quantity and speed and the degree of change have accelerated.

It is not always easy to be open to the unfamiliar, to forms so new that they bewilder. It is comforting, however, to learn about the audiences of the past, for they had their problems, too. Sometimes an innovation strikes at such a perfect moment – surely *La Sylphide* was one – that all observers recognize its claim to greatness. But sometimes a battle is necessary. How hard John

Martin had to fight to make his contemporaries see the point of the modern dance. Here, as we read about the failures and the successes, and about the failures that were later successes, we begin to cultivate the acumen to discern the place of the dance we have just seen within the whole picture of the evolution of the art. History does not tell us what to like, but it does give us the means to make intelligent choices.

This book is limited to the story of theatrical dance in the western world, which is already a great deal to manage in some 200 pages. The time restriction is dictated by the available evidence; only from the era of the court ballet do we have a continuous flow of documents to tell us about the development of theatrical dance. The geographical restriction is something else, for the situation of dance beyond America and Europe has presented a remarkably different picture.

Western dance has been characterized by change; gradual at first, then increasingly rapid. In Asia and Africa, however, stability has been the norm. There dance has served to define the rituals that mark the stages of the life cycle; it has been a medium of social cohesion for the community, perceived as a model of moral values, a symbol of the achievement of harmony with the physical and spiritual environment. In such societies tradition is sacred; the ways of the ancestors are respected and preserved.

Now these societies are hearing the western message of change. Companies have toured; sometimes dancers have remained to teach, offering instruction in techniques that are enticing in their strangeness. Television has spread the ideas of ballet and tap and modern and post-modern dance for all to adapt or absorb. Whether the non-western countries can take ideas from these new forms and still maintain the integrity of their national traditions remains to be seen. Perhaps this book can serve them, as it serves us, in elucidating the present by exploring its relation to the past.

As the varieties of dance proliferate, the situation becomes increasingly complex and challenging. Susan Au can meet the challenge because she has prepared herself assiduously. A tireless researcher and meticulous scholar, she has, nevertheless, not restricted her experience to archives and museums. In fact, she is equally at home in the dance classroom and the theatre auditorium. It is this essential combination of thinking and doing, of reading and viewing, that enables her to make us see dance history as a living panorama, a vivid tradition that informs and illuminates our experience of dance today.

Selma Jeanne Cohen

2 A ballet class at the Paris Opéra, painted c.1876 by Edgar Degas. The teacher is the aged Jules Perrot, joint choreographer of Giselle in 1841 and in his youth a famous dancer. See pages 52–3.

CHAPTER ONE

A Most Obedient Servant

A 20th-century observer would be hard put to recognize the art form we call ballet in the French court ballets of the 16th and 17th centuries. The earliest of these performances preceded the invention of the proscenium stage and were presented in large chambers with most of the audience seated on tiers or galleries on three sides of the dancing floor. Since the majority of the spectators viewed the performers from above, most of their attention was focused on the 'figures' or floor patterns traced by the dancers as they moved about. The figured dance or horizontal dance, as it was called, consisted largely of geometric forms, often overlaid with symbolic meanings. They were almost always danced by single-sex groups rather than by men and women in couples.

The dancers in the earliest ballets were not the highly skilled professionals of today. Instead, they were usually noble amateurs, often led by the king or queen. In contrast to today's ballet dancers they would seem very earthbound, for the steps and movements they executed were derived from the social dances of the time, which emphasized decorum, grace and elegance rather than feats of strength or agility. The dancers' costumes, based on the fashionable court dress of the day, were meant primarily to impress spectators with their opulence and inventiveness; freedom of movement was only a secondary consideration.

Lengthy performances and a leisurely pace were characteristic of many of these entertainments: beginning late at night, they went on for as many as four or five hours. Early court ballets tended to have a processional flavour, with decorated cars or large pieces of movable scenery, resembling the floats in modern-day parades, carrying on dancers, singers and musicians.

These courtly spectacles, alien as they might seem to our eyes, were nevertheless the ancestors of the art of ballet. Behind them lay a long tradition of court festivals and entertainments, reaching back to the processions and mummeries of the Middle Ages. In contrast to these medieval entertainments, the court ballet served secular rather than religious functions, frequently combining political motives with the desire for pleasure and diversion. It existed primarily for the ruling class, which supplied a large proportion of the performers as well as the audience. The different components of a court ballet – dance, poetry, music and design – were usually

3 The setting for the Ballet Comique de la Reine Louise *(1581), as shown in the frontispiece to its libretto. The scenery included a mass of golden clouds, concealing singers (left), the garden and palace of Circe (centre background) and the grove of Pan (right).*

coordinated by an organizer who supervised the entire production. The collaborators could be noblemen or professionals, but they all joined in expressing the aristocratic point of view. In short, the court ballet was a carefully calculated mixture of art, politics and entertainment; its chief purpose was to glorify the State, which could be symbolized, as in the time of Louis XIV, by the reigning monarch.

Both France and Italy contributed to the development of the court ballet. The courts of both countries had long delighted in grandiose spectacles combining, in different proportions, costumed and masked performers, fantastically decorated cars, songs and instrumental music, speeches and verses, dances, mock battles and jousts. These entertainments were presented between courses of a banquet or acts of a play; they accompanied royal entries into a town or celebrated special events such as aristocratic weddings. Catherine de' Medici, who is said to have brought her taste for dancing to France from her native Italy, included dancing in many of the royal entertainments she commanded; an early example is *Le Paradis d'Amour* (1572), presented at the wedding of her daughter Marguerite de Valois and Henry of Navarre. This dance, performed by twelve ladies dressed as nymphs, was itself part of an elaborate mock-combat that concluded with a display of fireworks.

The court ballet, however, did not simply evolve out of the traditions of its predecessors. To some degree it was a conscious invention, strongly influenced by current ideas on the arts. The Académie de Musique et de la Poésie, founded in Paris in 1570 by the poet Jean-Antoine de Baïf (1532–89) and the composer Thibault de Courville, exerted a particularly powerful influence on the development of the court ballet. Baïf and his followers wished to resuscitate the poetry, music and dance of the ancient world. The Académie's concept of an art form that would fuse all the arts was to some extent realized by the composite form of the court ballet, which united poetry, music, dance and design.

The court ballet had particularly close ties to the literature of its time. Most ballet themes derived from literary sources, and the ballets themselves included spoken or sung verses which were called *récits*. Printed librettos containing these verses, together with explanations of the ballet's intentions and symbolism, were often distributed to the audience. Symbolism and allegory were important components of the court ballet, as they were in the art and literature of the period. Persons, objects and events were more often than not subject to multiple levels of interpretation. Manuals such as Cesare Ripa's *Iconologia* (1593) provided an abundant source of visual symbols or 'emblems'. The court ballet was itself an emblem: in its union of the arts it represented the harmony of the celestial spheres, as manifested on earth in the

4 *Like most court ballets, the* Ballet des Polonais *(1573) was followed by a ball that mingled performers and onlookers. Musicians dressed as Apollo and the Muses accompanied the dancing from an artificial Parnassus (left).*

government of the ruler. In addition, the court ballet used emblems in more concrete forms: as figures of the dance, characters, or elements of the scenery or costumes.

Furthermore, the 16th and 17th centuries believed that the court ballet was more than a frivolous diversion. Like the other arts, it could exert a real effect on the lives of those who watched and participated in it. Dancing in general was considered a means of socializing the individual and drawing him into harmony with the group, and formed an important part of the education of a gentleman. Most court ballets ended with a 'grand ballet', celebrating the return of concord or harmony within the context of the ballet; this was followed by a ball in which everyone joined, symbolically drawing both spectators and performers into accord with the ideas expressed by the performance.

One of the first works to be recognized as a true court ballet was the *Ballet des Polonais*, staged in 1573 to honour the Polish ambassadors who were visiting Paris upon the accession of Henry of Anjou to the throne of Poland.

13

Commissioned by Catherine de' Medici, it was organized by her compatriot Baldassarino da Belgiojoso, who had taken the French name of Balthasar de Beaujoyeulx (fl. *c.*1555–87). Its highlight was an hour-long ballet danced by sixteen ladies representing the provinces of France. This ballet consisted of many intricate, interlacing figures, which the ladies were said to have performed faultlessly.

Beaujoyeulx was also responsible for an even more ambitious project, the *Ballet Comique de la Reine Louise*, which was presented in 1581 as part of the wedding festivities for the Duc de Joyeuse and Marguerite of Lorraine, the sister of Queen Louise. The *Ballet Comique* was the first court spectacle to apply the principles of Baïf's Académie by integrating dance, poetry, music and design to convey a unified dramatic plot. Beaujoyeulx took charge of the choreography as well as the general organization of the ballet. The plot was derived from an episode in Homer's *Odyssey*, the encounter with the enchantress Circe, who transformed men into animals. In Beaujoyeulx's reworking, this story was given added meanings. Circe, representing man's baser passions – his animal nature – was defeated with the help of Minerva, the goddess of wisdom; Pan, symbolizing the forces of nature; and Jupiter, the omnipotent ruler of the gods.

At the beginning of the ballet a courtier playing a 'fugitive gentleman' cast himself at the feet of the king, Henry III, to beg his aid in resisting the machinations of Circe. This was not merely as an appeal to the king's vanity. Like the wedding itself, the ballet was meant to reconcile warring factions and heal the religious strife that had torn the country. Circe was a symbol of civil war, while the restoration of peace and concord at the end of the ballet represented the country's hopes for the future. The king was invoked in his own person as the means of realizing these hopes.

The ballet's choreography consisted of figured dances; Queen Louise and her ladies, dressed as naiads, were borne in on a three-tiered fountain to dance with twelve pages. Forty geometric figures, danced by naiads and dryads, comprised the concluding grand ballet.

The rise of the court ballet in France paralleled the birth of opera in Italy. In Florence the Camerata, a group of poets and composers comparable to Baïf's Académie, sought a similar fusion of the arts. The development of the court ballet also coincided with the opening of the first public theatres in France and the rise of the great French playwrights Corneille and Racine. Although the court ballet shared certain tendencies and influences with contemporary opera and drama, it placed more emphasis upon dancing than the opera, which tended to reserve dances for the interludes between acts, and was more flexible in form than classical drama, since it did not have to observe restrictions such as the three unities of time, place and action.

5 *Grotesque dances provided a lively contrast to the stately dignity of the court ballet. In this scene from the* Ballet de la Délivrance de Renaud *(1617), the monsters summoned up by the enchantress Armida have turned into comical old people.*

As the 17th century began, the court ballet started to diversify both its form and its subject matter. In the *Ballet d'Alcine* (1610), the text was sung rather than declaimed; this was the first time that musical recitative, which had been developed by the Camerata, was used in France. *Alcine* also introduced a new element of comedy, which was to become increasingly important in the court ballet. For example, a grotesque dance was performed by twelve knights whom the enchantress Alcine had transformed into objects such as windmills, flowerpots and bass viols.

The court ballet also began to draw inspiration from new sources. Chivalric romances, which were popular in the literature of the time, came into favour early in the 17th century. The *Ballet de la Délivrance de Renaud* (1617), an important example of this theme, demonstrates how the court ballet could be turned to political purposes. Inspired by Tasso's *Gerusalemme Liberata*, it resembled the *Ballet Comique de la Reine Louise* in its story of a man's deliverance from the toils of an evil sorceress. In this ballet, however, the theme was pointedly applied to the actual situation of the nation. Louis XIII, having recently freed himself of the regency of his mother, Marie de' Medici, and the various court conspiracies against him, was anxious to establish his authority as king, and chose the court ballet as a memorable means of announcing his intentions.

15

Reflecting real events in allegorical terms, the ballet depicted the reclamation of the hero Renaud (Tasso's Rinaldo) from the life of aimless luxury and frivolity imposed upon him by the enchantress Armida. It included scenes of magic and comedy, both of which were popular with audiences of the time: for example, Armida, enraged by Renaud's defection, summoned up demons in the shapes of crayfish, tortoises, and snails. To her chagrin, however, these creatures turned into ridiculous old people. The climax of the ballet was a scene of celebration in the golden pavilion of the crusader Godefroy de Bouillon, played by the king, who led his lords in a grand ballet. Louis also played the role of the spirit of fire, which was associated with both divinity and purification.

Although these works used a unified narrative structure, later productions placed less and less emphasis on dramatic continuity. In the *ballet-mascarade*, the dances, preceded by a spoken *récit* or a song, were tenuously connected by a slender plot. Similar in form was the *ballet à entrées*. Each *entrée* was structured like a *ballet mascarade*, with an opening *récit* or song followed by dances. A series of *entrées* was usually linked by a common theme: The *Ballet des Voleurs* (1624), for example, featured nocturnally inclined characters such as Night, the stars, thieves and serenaders. Each *entrée* involved a relatively small number of performers, usually between three and six.

The episodical nature of these two forms required less planning and rehearsal, and therefore less expense, than the dramatic ballets. The taste for ballet spread to the bourgeoisie, who produced these ballets on a modest scale in private houses in imitation of the ballets presented by the king and his court. M. de Saint-Hubert, whose book *La Manière de composer et faire réussir les ballets* [*How to Compose a Successful Ballet*] was published in 1641, stated that a royal ballet usually consisted of thirty *entrées*, a 'fine ballet' of at least twenty, and a small ballet of ten to twelve.

Between 1620 and 1636, satirical ballets that mocked the manners and pretensions of their time became particularly popular. Among their favourite targets were professions and national types. In the *Ballet des Fées de la Fôret de Saint-Germain* (1625), the fairies' retainers include roulette players, Spanish dancers, warriors, headhunters and doctors. The *Ballet Royal du grand bal de la Douairière de Billebahaut* (1626) took place at a pompous reception given by the aged and ugly dowager and her fiancé, Fanfan de Sotteville. The international guest list included Atabalipa, the king of Cuzco; the Great Turk; the grand Cacique, mounted on an elephant; and the Great Cham, on a camel. The costumes, designed by Daniel Rabel, struck a fine balance between fantasy and authenticity, but they already displayed a taste for caricature that was to grow increasingly pronounced in the course of the century.

6 *Among the ridiculous guests who appeared in the* Ballet Royal du grand bal de la Douairière de Billebahaut *(1626) was the Grand Cham, a monarch of Asia, riding on a camel.*

These ballets encouraged the growth of pantomimic dances, which contrasted with the more formalized figured dances in their emphasis upon characterization. These dances, however, usually portrayed strongly marked types rather than individuals. The customary wearing of masks suppressed facial expression, although the masks worn for pantomime dances were generally individualized to help identify the characters. In the figured dances of the grand ballets, where uniformity was more important than individuality, identical black masks were worn.

Pantomimic dances often contained acrobatic elements that placed considerable demands upon the dancer's technical skill. These dances were usually performed by professionals, commoners rather than nobles, recruited from street entertainers, travelling players, acrobats and the like. With the passage of the years, the court ballet became less exclusively aristocratic. Parts were assigned on the basis of ability rather than rank, and nobles and commoners mingled in the dances without regard for precedence.

Towards the end of the reign of Louis XIII, Cardinal Richelieu again gave the court ballet a political bent, this time employing it to consolidate the power of the king. In order to do so, Richelieu blended ancient mythology and more recent events such as Louis's military victories. The names of mythical gods and heroes were invoked to strengthen and add legitimacy to the king's claims; Louis was often called the French Hercules. He was also associated with the sun, a symbol more often linked with his successor, Louis XIV.

The opening of the *Ballet de la Prospérité des armes de la France* (1641), Richelieu's last contribution to the court ballet, showed France in a state of harmony which was disrupted by Pluto, the god of the underworld, and his minions. The ballet then reenacted various French triumphs over the Spanish, both on land and at sea. The gods themselves were shown paying tribute to Louis, and the ballet closed on a self-congratulatory note, celebrating the return of concord and abundance to France.

This ballet was performed on the proscenium stage of the theatre of the Palais-Royal, which Richelieu had had built for his personal use. The introduction of the proscenium as a frame for the action had far-reaching effects on the art of ballet. It served as a distancing device between the performers and the audience, which was now called upon to admire rather than participate. The figured dances of the past lost favour as the audience's new viewpoint sharpened its appreciation of the 'perilous leaps', turns, and other feats of the professional dancers. The physical structure of the proscenium stage also allowed the development of increasingly elaborate stage effects, created by a variety of ingenious machines. Italian designers, foremost among them the Francini brothers, Gaspare Vigarani and his son Carlo, and Giacomo Torelli led the way in French stage design.

The French court ballet reached its height during the reign of Louis XIV, whose very birth had been celebrated by the *Ballet de la Félicité* of 1639. The young king, who made his debut as a dancer in the *Ballet de Cassandre* in 1651, enjoyed the position of first dancer of the realm until his retirement in 1670. One of his favourite roles was that of the god Apollo, who was closely associated with solar symbolism. As the *Roi Soleil* or Sun King, Louis became the human embodiment of the brilliance and splendour of France.

The court ballet of his reign gloried in variety. The favourite themes and personages of the past decades – the mythological deities, the chivalric heroes,

7,8 Symmetrical geometric forms were an important choreographic device in the court ballets. The central figure in this drawing (below, left) of an unknown ballet of c.1660 may represent Louis XIV. The king is shown right in costume for a court ballet of 1665. He carries a miniature sun, his personal symbol, signifying the brilliance of his reign.

the idealized shepherds and shepherdesses of the pastorals, the grotesque characters and ethnic types of the satirical ballets – not only co-existed but often mingled in extravagant spectacles.

Such a spectacle was the *Ballet de la Nuit* of 1653, in which forty-five *entrées*, divided into four parts or 'vigils', provided a detailed picture of the landscape of the night. It included personified abstractions such as Night and the four elements; mythological figures such as the goddesses Venus and Diana; and characters from Ariosto's *Orlando Furioso*, who gathered to watch a ballet within a ballet, the *Marriage of Thetis*. Witches, werewolves and other demonic creatures celebrated a black sabbath. The more 'realistic' characters included gypsies, shepherds driving home their flocks, lamplighters, thieves, counterfeiters, beggars and bogus cripples. The coming of day was heralded by the Rising Sun, played by Louis in the first of his many impersonations of the sun god. He led the final grand ballet in which personifications of Honour, Grace, Love, Valour, Victory, Favour, Renown and Peace united to do him homage.

A number of creative men lent their talents to the production of Louis's court ballets, among them the poet Isaac de Benserade, the composer and dancer Jean-Baptiste Lully, the designers Torelli, Vigarani and Henry de Gissey and the dancing-master Pierre Beauchamp.

Louis XIV was not alone in his use of spectacle to create an aura of divinity about the king. In England the masque, a composite art form akin to the court ballet, served a similar function. The masque had originated late in the 16th century, like the court ballet, but was given definitive form by the architect Inigo Jones and the poet and playwright Ben Jonson, who first collaborated in 1605, on *The Masque of Blackness*, and continued to work together until 1631.

The masque, like the court ballet, employed numerous emblems and allegories. Jones was convinced that visual images could express moral and philosophical truths better than words and his talents as designer, architect and engineer enabled him to give physical shape to his ideas. He believed that a successful stage illusion should be nicely calculated to evoke wonder in the viewer without permitting him to forget that this marvel was the result of man's inventive genius. Jonson, on the other hand, felt that the 'invention' of the masque (the motivating ideas contributed by the poet), should not be overshadowed by mere spectacle. This disagreement eventually led to a rift between the two.

The masque in general revealed a strong belief in man's ability to control his world. The image of the garden, representing nature tamed and cultivated by man, frequently recurred. During the 1630s, when Charles I ruled as absolute monarch of England and, like Louis XIV, performed leading roles in the court masques, he was always portrayed as wise, just, benevolent, virtuous and courageous – in short, worthy in every way of the divine right to kingship that he claimed. In the masques he brought order out of disorder, as he hoped to do in real life.

Elements antithetical to Charles and his rule were portrayed symbolically in the 'anti-masque', which denoted not a separate art form but a mimed or danced episode, usually grotesque in nature, that preceded the evening's main performance. Most anti-masques were probably executed by professional dancers. Some of the characters represented seem relatively innocuous today, such as 'mad lovers', straying pilgrims, and pygmies, but more traditional villains such as witches, furies and vices were also depicted.

Among the great masques of the 1630s was Jonson's *Love's Triumph through Callipolis* (1631). In its opening scene Callipolis, an idealized city of beauty and virtue, was cleansed of such unwelcome elements as the 'whining', 'fantastical', and 'melancholy' lovers. In contrast, the king personified Heroic Love, to which all men must aspire. A scene representing a sea crossing alluded both to the love goddess Venus, who had risen from the sea, and to Britain's maritime power. King and court alike paid tribute to the queen, Henrietta Maria, whom Jonson's verses lauded as the 'centre of proportion, sweetness, grace'. At the conclusion of the masque, Venus herself descended

9,10 The English court masque reached its peak of elaboration in the reign of Charles I, under the direction of the architect and designer Inigo Jones. On the left is Jones's design for 'a fantastical lover' in the antimasque that opened Love's Triumph through Callipolis; *on the right is a design for Queen Henrietta Maria's costume in* Chloridia. *Both masques were written by Ben Jonson in 1631.*

to face her earthly counterpart, Henrietta Maria, in a metaphorical declaration of love's power to unite heaven and earth.

More nationalistic in theme was *Coelum Britannicum* (1634), with its text by Thomas Carew, in which Jupiter himself sought to emulate Charles's court by re-creating it in heaven. Among the glories designed by Jones for this masque was the rise of an enormous mountain, bearing personifications of the kingdoms of England, Scotland and Ireland, and surmounted by the Genius of Great Britain, all celebrating the foundation of the British Empire.

Salmacida Spolia (1640), the last of the court masques, was far less optimistic in tone. Charles played the role of Philogenes, king of a troubled realm. The triumphal note of *Coelum Britannicum* gave way to a plea for unity and concord. The masque's text, written by Sir William Davenant, derived from the ancient myth of the spring Salmacis, which had the power to make men effeminate. In a nation torn by strife, however, conciliation had come to be looked upon as a virtue rather than a weakness.

The masque, like the court ballet, thus reflected to some extent the political life of its country. Unlike the court ballet, however, the masque did not survive the passing of the monarchy that it had served.

LE
TRIOMPHE
DE
L'AMOVR

Daniel Marot Sculp.

CHAPTER TWO

The Rise of Professionalism

As the 17th century progressed, ballet in France was gradually transformed from the diversion of noble amateurs into a professional art. Although professional dancers had initially been introduced into the court ballet to perform grotesque or acrobatic dances – those that were below a nobleman's dignity or above his level of proficiency – the court ballet's dependency on professionals waxed rather than waned with time, and professional dancers were much in demand. Despite the commonly held belief that female professional dancers did not appear until 1681, they actually began to perform prior to that date in the court ballets of Louis XIV. Among these dancers were Mademoiselle Vertpré, who danced opposite the king himself in the *Ballet de l'Impatience* (1661), and the Mademoiselles de Mollier, Girault and de la Faveur.

The audience's perception of the dancer began to alter as performing conditions changed. The proscenium stage created both physical and psychic distance between the performers and the spectators, who were no longer encouraged to identify with the former as they had been in the days when the court ballet was a symbolic means of creating unity among different factions. Professional dancers began to evolve technical feats that demanded a high degree of training and skill, such as pirouettes, cabrioles and entrechats (the last two are jumps in which the legs are beaten together in the air); more and more, the professional's achievements exceeded the range of even the most accomplished amateur.

The playwright Molière's *comédies-ballets*, introduced in 1661 with *Les Fâcheux*, may be viewed as a transitional form between the court ballet and the professional theatrical art that was developing. The invention of this form was said to be accidental: Molière (1622–73), having been invited to stage both a play and a ballet for a fête in honour of Louis XIV, found himself with too few dancers to meet his needs, and decided to combine the two in order to give the performers time to change their costumes and catch their breath. The result immediately won favour, and he went on to create a total of twelve *comédies-ballets* before his death in 1673. Molière's collaborators included the dancing-master Pierre Beauchamp (1631–c.1719), who created the dances for *Les Fâcheux*, and the composer Lully (1632–87), who first worked with him in 1664. Both men had already made names for themselves in the court ballets.

23

11 *Lully's ballet* Le Triomphe de l'Amour *(1681) was the occasion of the first appearance of female professional dancers on the stage of the Paris Opéra.*

The *comédies-ballets* closely linked dance and music with the action of the play. Their strong dramatic interest and continuity distinguished them from the court ballets of the day, in which the separate *entrées* were episodes related by little more than a common theme. The *comédies-ballets* required the dancers as well as the actors to take an active part in furthering the plot. In *Les Fâcheux*, the hero Eraste was plagued by a series of bores, including a group of bowlers who performed a dance incorporating movements from the sport. In *Le Bourgeois Gentilhomme* (1670), four tailors danced a minuet as they undressed Monsieur Jourdain (who was played by Molière himself) and arrayed him in his new finery; the aspiring gentleman then took lessons in two indisputably gentlemanly arts, fencing and dancing, and was enthroned as a Grand Mamamouchi in an elaborately choreographed 'Turkish' ritual.

As in the court ballet, both professionals and noblemen mingled in the *comédies-ballets*. Louis XIV himself played an Egyptian in *Le Mariage forcé* (1664), and made his last appearance on stage in *Les Amants magnifiques* (1670) in the roles of Neptune and Apollo. His retirement (necessitated, it is sometimes said, by his growing corpulence) signalled the close of the era of the amateur; possibly his courtiers felt that performing had lost much of its cachet once he had abandoned it.

Long before his retirement, however, Louis had taken a major step towards ensuring the future of ballet in France by granting letters patent to the Académie Royale de Danse in 1661. The aims of the Académie, which consisted of thirteen leading dancing-masters, centred on improving the quality of dance instruction and establishing 'scientific principles' for the art. The Académie was responsible for training dancers to perform in the king's ballets, preparing aspiring masters and sharpening the skills of existing ones, keeping a register of all Parisian masters and passing judgment on all new dances.

The Académie de Danse was not a performing group, unlike the shortlived Académie d'Opéra, established in 1669 under Pierre Perrin, who hoped to develop French opera by combining poetry and music. Perrin and his associates managed to stage only one production before artistic and financial problems forced them to abandon their enterprise. Lully, who had been awaiting his chance, persuaded the king to transfer the functions of Perrin's group to a third organization, the Académie Royale de Musique et de Danse, founded in 1672 with Lully as its director and Beauchamp as its dancing-master.

The Italian-born Lully had risen to prominence in the French court thanks to his talents as dancer, violinist and composer. As the head of the Académie de Musique (later known familiarly as the Paris Opéra), he established a virtual monopoly over the French musical theatre that lasted until his death in

1687. His efforts helped transfer the art of ballet from the court to the theatre. With the foundation of the Académie he began to build up a troupe of professional dancers, whom he initially recruited from the pupils of Parisian masters. At first this troupe consisted solely of men; although female professional dancers had appeared in the court ballets, none was admitted to Lully's troupe, and female roles were played by boys in travesty.

Ballet and opera had not yet evolved into separate art forms at this time, and most of the works produced by Lully's troupe contained varying proportions of both dance and vocal music. The *tragédie-lyrique*, a new theatrical form which he developed in collaboration with Beauchamp and the librettist Philippe Quinault (1635–88), used both dance and song to convey a plot comparable to the tragedies of Corneille and Racine. *Cadmus et Hermione* (1673), the first of these, included a chaconne, a dance of golden statues and dances of sacrifice and celebration. Lully took a keen interest in the dramatic content of these works and sometimes devised passages of mime himself, but much of the action was conveyed by the singers. This was necessitated, in part, by a shortage of good dancers. Also, dancers still wore masks, which eliminated the possibility of facial expression.

12, 13 *Left, Jean-Baptiste Lully, a dancer as well as a composer, dominated the Paris Opéra from 1672 until his death in 1687. Under his leadership, ballet and opera made the transition from court entertainments to professional arts.* Right, *Feuillet notation was first used in the 1700s to record both theatrical and ballroom dances. Today it often forms the basis for reconstructing dances of this period.*

In addition to his choreographic work, Beauchamp codified the existing ballet technique. He is credited with identifying the five canonical positions of the feet, upon which all ballet steps are based; they were published in Pierre Rameau's *Le Maitre à Danser* [*The Dancing Master*] in 1725. The turned-out position of the legs and feet was used in both theatrical and social dancing, although it was less extreme in the latter. The ninety degree turnout that later became standard for ballet dancers was first used by professionals in grotesque dances.

Beauchamp also systematized the method of teaching dance, and under his tutelage the dancers of the Paris Opéra gained in facility. In 1681 female professional dancers appeared for the first time as part of the company, 11 dancing in the ballet *Le Triomphe de l'Amour*. These four pioneering dancers were led by Mademoiselle de Lafontaine (*c*.1655–*c*.1738), who became the Opéra's first principal ballerina. The female dance style of the period was more sedate than the male, partly because of the restrictions of costume and partly because of the demands of decorum. Both sexes, however, were expected to display ease and effortlessness and to conceal physical exertion. Elegance and harmony were the hallmarks of good dancing.

In the late 1670s Louis XIV encouraged Beauchamp to devise a system of dance notation. However, Beauchamp himself never published this system, which was subsequently published and popularized by Raoul Auger Feuillet (*c*.1650–1709), whose name has been given to the system. Feuillet's book *Chorégraphie* – the term 'choreography' then denoted dance notation rather than the art of making dances – was first published in 1700 and went through many editions and translations. It contained diagrams of various steps, many 13 of which are recognizable today, and records of social and theatrical dances choreographed by Louis Pécour (*c*.1653–1729) and Feuillet himself, which were supplemented annually by newly notated dances.

Beauchamp retired in 1687, the year of Lully's death. He was succeeded by his former student Pécour, who had made his debut as a dancer in 1673. During Pécour's long tenure as balletmaster, a number of notable dancers rose to fame, among them Michel Blondy, Claude Balon (for many years erroneously called Jean Balon by historians), Marie-Thérèse Perdou de Subligny and Françoise Prévost. In 1713 Louis XIV issued a decree that established a permanent troupe of dancers at the Opéra, and officially created a school of dance associated with it.

Pécour made his greatest contribution as a choreographer in collaboration with the composer André Campra (1660–1744), who developed a new form 29 called the *opéra-ballet*. Although it was, like its predecessors, a combination of dancing and vocal music, its novelty lay in its loose construction, for each act was an independent entity that could stand alone. In contrast to the *tragédies-*

14, 15 Two stars of the Paris Opéra: left, *Marie-Thérèse Perdou de Subligny, one of the first female dancers to win acclaim;* right, *Claude Balon, who is sometimes said to have given his name to the quality called* ballon *in dancing, which signifies the dancer's ability to jump with lightness and ease.*

lyriques, the themes of the *opéras-ballets* were lighter in nature, and were often set in exotic locales. Programmes made up of the best-liked acts from several different *opéras-ballets* were frequently presented. Possibly the most famous example of this form was Jean–Philippe Rameau's *Les Indes Galantes* (1735), which had a libretto by Louis Fuzelier and decor by Jean Nicholas Servandoni. This work, composed of a prologue and three (later four) *entrées*, depicted love stories in the exotic climes of Turkey, Peru, Persia and North America.

Although by the early 18th century dance had gained an important place in the productions of the Paris Opéra, it still served a primarily decorative function. Despite their increasing technical proficiency, dancers were seldom called upon to use their expressive potential. Yet, although the *opéra-ballet* retained its popularity until well into the century, a new concept of dance was shaping, one that would draw upon the inherent expressiveness of movement to make dancers, in their own way, as eloquent as the singers and actors of ballet's formative years.

CHAPTER THREE

The Development of the Ballet d'Action

The 18th century was an age of brilliant dancers, yet it was also a time when both dancers and choreographers began to seek something beyond the mere display of technique. Dance, they felt, should be more than an ornament or even an object of wonder; it should convey some meaning to the viewer. The problem of how to achieve this preoccupied many choreographers and led to the evolution of the *ballet d'action*, which unfolded a story purely in terms of movement.

Ballet had already made some progress toward this goal by the beginning of the century. Although it still had much in common with social dancing, it was beginning to escape the constraints of decorum imposed by the polite world. The professional dancer was no longer required to preserve a gentlemanly demeanour; instead, as the dramatic dimension of ballet grew, he was often called upon to display emotions that could seldom if ever be expressed in public life.

Although ballet had not been entirely devoid of dramatic content in the 16th and 17th centuries, this aspect frequently had been overshadowed by its other functions (such as the political propaganda of the court ballet) or by the presence of other arts, such as poetry or vocal music, which were given the task of revealing the action. Early in the 18th century, however, theoreticians began to propose a type of dance that could stand on its own, fulfilling in itself the narrative functions once taken by poetry or song.

Many of these ideas were inspired, as in the days of Baïf's Académie, by current notions of ancient Greek and Roman dance and pantomime. Writing in 1710, Pierre-Jean Burette drew upon Plato, Aristotle and other ancient thinkers as support for his belief that dance could express actions and emotions through rhythmic gestures. Like Baïf and his followers, Burette compared dance to the other arts, describing it as animated painting. The Abbé Jean-Baptiste du Bos, in his *Réflexions critiques sur la poésie et sur la peinture* (1719), criticized the dance of his day for its empty subservience to gracefulness and contrasted it unfavourably with the expressive gestures of the Greek choruses and the Roman pantomimes, who knew how to convey meanings through their movements.

Charles Batteux expanded upon the idea of imitation in *Les Beaux Arts reduits à un même principe* (1746). Imitation, as understood by Batteux and

16 Marie Camargo, one of the 18th century's greatest ballerinas, was admired for her dazzling virtuosity, especially in the beaten jumps called entrechats. Nicolas Lancret's painting places her not on stage but in the idealized setting of a park.

other 18th-century aestheticians, was not a matter of slavish mimicry nor yet of slice-of-life realism; instead, the artist used his creative powers to represent the object according to his notion of things as they should be. Yet imitation could not move the spectator nor have any meaning unless it had a firm basis in real life: human actions and emotions.

Practical examples of the use of movement for expressive purposes could be found in the popular theatre of the time, particularly the Italian *commedia dell'arte* and the pantomimes of the French and English fairground theatres, which had a tradition of incorporating dance, often of an acrobatic or virtuosic nature, into their narratives. Both freely employed bold effects of gesture and 'body language' to make their points clear to their audiences.

Theory and practice were linked by the English choreographer John Weaver (1673–1760). In his *Essay Towards an History of Dancing* (1712), the first full-length history of the art published in England, he declared that the dance of the ancient world was superior to that of his own day by virtue of its greater expressive capacity. Yet he believed this could be remedied and that theatrical dancing could again be made capable of conveying meanings to the viewer through movement.

His ideas were applied in *The Loves of Mars and Venus* (1717), which he described in its libretto as 'A Dramatick Entertainment of Dancing, Attempted in Imitation of the Pantomimes of the Ancient Greeks and Romans'. In this work, presented at the Drury Lane theatre in London, he attempted the then unprecedented task of communicating the action of the piece and the personalities of the characters through poses, gestures and dancing, without relying on a spoken or sung text. To express his meanings, he used a combination of formalized, conventional gestures, such as striking the left hand with the right to signify anger, and more naturalistic gestures such as averting the face to express detestation.

The story of this ballet ultimately derived from ancient mythology, although Weaver's immediate source was P. A. Motteux's play *The Loves of Mars and Venus* (1696). In contrast to many later dramatic ballets, the plot was not a complicated one. Venus, the goddess of love and beauty, rejects the admiring advances of her blacksmith husband Vulcan (played by Weaver himself) with a mixture of coquetry and contempt. His love turns to jealousy and he vows to revenge himself. A meeting between Venus and her lover, the war god Mars, sharply contrasts his masculine strength with her feminine softness and delicacy. Vulcan traps the guilty lovers under a net and triumphantly summons the other gods to witness their disgrace. But he is at last persuaded to forgive them, and the gods and goddesses join in a Grand Dance. Venus was danced by Hester Santlow (c.1690–1773), an English dancer famed for her beauty and her skill both as a dancer and an actress. The role of Mars, credited in the libretto to 'Mr Dupré, Senior', may have been performed by Louis Dupré (1697–1744), a renowned French exponent of the so called 'noble style' of dancing, which emphasized the qualities of grace, precision and majesty. *The Loves of Mars and Venus* was popular enough to inspire a parody version by John Rich, the director of the theatre at Lincoln's Inns Fields and Weaver's chief competitor. He developed a highly successful form of entertainment by injecting harlequinades between the scenes of serious plays. Unlike Weaver, he combined dialogue and songs with the dancing and mime in his works.

In France an early example of dramatic dance was presented at the château of Sceaux as part of the festivities sponsored by the Duchesse du Maine in 1714. Two stars of the Paris Opéra, Françoise Prévost (c.1680–1741) and Claude Balon (1676–1739), performed a scene from the last act of Corneille's tragedy *Les Horaces*, in which the Roman patrician Horatius is reproached by his sister Camilla for the murder of her lover, a member of the rival party of the Curiati. The scene was played wholly in pantomime and was said to have moved the spectators to tears. However, it remained an isolated event and no attempt appears to have been made to imitate it at the Paris Opéra.

Prévost, however, retained some degree of interest in the dramatic possibilities of dance. In her famous solo *Les Caractères de la Danse*, performed to a suite of dances composed by Jean Ferry Rebel in 1715, she portrayed a series of lovers of various ages and both sexes. The *bourrée* depicted a shepherdess who prays to Amour in hopes of winning the heart of a disdainful shepherd; the *menuet*, a twelve-year-old girl who wants her mother to fall asleep so she can meet her lover; the *passepied*, a man who hopes to win back a neglectful mistress through a pretence of indifference. The dance closed with a *musette* by a young woman who, being perfectly happy in love, pays homage to Amour.

Prévost taught this well-received solo to her two most famous female students, Marie Camargo (1710–70) and Marie Sallé (1707–56). These two dancers came to symbolize two divergent approaches to ballet. Camargo, who made her debut at the Paris Opéra in this dance in 1726, was a brilliant technician, excelling in beaten steps such as entrechats and cabrioles. Audiences were charmed with her sprightliness and vivacity. Female dancers' skirts were being shortened at the time of her career, and this allowed her sparkling footwork to be better seen. Her growing popularity aroused the jealousy of Prévost, who placed her in the corps de ballet until the day that Camargo unexpectedly stepped into the place of a missing male dancer and improvised a dazzling solo. After that, her position as a principal ballerina was secure. She began to study with male teachers who sharpened her attack and perhaps taught her some of their feats as well.

16

Sallé, in contrast, devoted her career to exploring the dramatic potential of dance. As a child dancer in the fairground theatres of Paris and London, she had the opportunity to observe the pantomimes presented there. She may have seen Weaver's *The Loves of Mars and Venus* while performing in London in 1717. Like Camargo, she learned Prévost's solo *Les Caractères de la Danse*, but adapted it as a pas de deux for herself and a male partner, the better to bring out the emotional interchanges of each dance. Although she performed sporadically at the Paris Opéra, she found an even more congenial atmosphere in London, where she danced in the operas of George Frideric Handel. The first female choreographer of note, she attempted a number of innovations.

Pygmalion (1734), her best known work, was first performed at the Covent Garden theatre in London. In this ballet, based on the Greek myth of a sculptor whose beautiful statue comes to life, her choreography gave the impression of a danced conversation. Dancing the role of the statue, she tried to give greater veracity to the piece by dressing in simple Greek robes rather than the corset, petticoats and panniers commonly worn by female dancers of the period. Instead of donning an elaborate wig, she let her hair flow loosely down her back. *Pygmalion* made Sallé the toast of two cities. Her highly successful season in London was followed by performances in Paris, attended by the French king and queen. Unfortunately, her attempts at costume reform were not imitated until much later in the century.

Sallé retired from the public stage in 1740, at the early age of thirty-three. Her decision to retire is sometimes attributed to the rise of Barbara Campanini (1721–99), called La Barbarina, whose virtuosic abilities eclipsed even Camargo. Gifted as an actress as well as a dancer, Barbarina danced Sallé's role of the statue in a restaging of *Pygmalion* in Berlin in 1745. Among the dancers in this production was the young Jean Georges Noverre (1727–1810), later to become the century's most aggressive proponent of the *ballet d'action.*

By the mid-century a number of choreographers were investigating the expressive and dramatic possibilities of dance. In Paris Jean-Baptiste de Hesse (1705–79), working at the Théâtre Italien and at Madame de Pompadour's private theatre in Versailles, trained his dancers to move in an expressive style that was influenced by both pantomime and the *commedia dell'arte*. He treated both serious and comic subjects, but although the characters in his comic ballets were often drawn from the lower classes – servants, soldiers, farmers, shepherds and the like – they were portrayed in an idealized rather than a realistic fashion.

Similar experiments were being made in Vienna by Franz Anton Hilverding (1710–68), who may have seen the work of Sallé while studying

17 Though portrayed here in the conventional dancer's garb of the period, Marie Sallé is best remembered for her attempt to introduce more authentic costumes in Pygmalion *(1734).*

18 Hogarth used dotted lines to indicate the high jumps of La Barbarina and Desnoyer, two popular virtuoso dancers of his time, in his satirical print The Charmers of the Age *(1782).*

Le Turc Généreux

*Ballet Pantomime executé à Vienne sur le Teatre près de la Cour le 26 Avril, 1758.
Presenté à S.M. Mons. le Comte de Durazzo Conseiller intime actuel de L.L. M.M. I.I. et R.R. et Surintendant
general des Plaisirs et Spectacles &. &. par Bocc-Belotti dit Canaletto Peintre de S.M. le Roi de Pol. Elec. de Saxe & &. 1759.*

19 In this scene from Le Turc Généreux *(1758) the heroine begs her Turkish master to spare her lover. Franz Anton Hilverding's choreography required the dancers to express emotions with their whole bodies.*

in Paris between 1734 and 1736. During the 1740s he began to create dramatic ballets, many of which were inspired by the stories of mythological lovers: Orpheus and Eurydice, Venus and Adonis, Diana and Endymion, Ariadne and Bacchus. His reworking of *Le Turc Généreux* (1758) from Rameau's *Les Indes Galantes* was commemorated in a print that has helped ensure its fame. As the print suggests, Hilverding's choreography employed the entire body, not merely the face and arms, to express emotions. Like de Hesse in Paris, he trained the Viennese dancers to move in this new style.

Hilverding's heavy duties as court choreographer required him to employ a series of assistants. The most important of these was Gaspare Angiolini (1731–1803), who took over his post in Vienna when, in 1758, Hilverding was invited to St Petersburg by the Czarina Elisabeth. Although Hilverding took many of his own leading dancers with him, he did much to develop the talents of the Russian dancers. He also tried to incorporate Russian themes into some of his productions, notably *Virtue's Refuge*, which lauded Russia as the 'Defender of Virtue'. He returned to Vienna in 1764 and in the following

20 Inigo Jones strikes a note of Oriental sumptuousness in his costume design for the Daughter of Night in The Masque of Blackness *(1605).*

year staged for the court *Le Triomphe de l'Amour*, in which the young Marie Antoinette performed with her brothers Ferdinand and Maximilian.

Meanwhile, Angiolini had continued Hilverding's interest in dramatic dance. In collaboration with the composer Gluck and the librettist Raniero di Calzabigi, he produced *Don Juan ou le Festin de Pierre* (1761), in which he attempted to raise expressive dance to new heights by representing a strong, almost horrific sequence of events. The plot (which was adapted by Mozart for his opera *Don Giovanni*) depicted Don Juan's murder of the Commandant, who had interrupted his tryst with the Commandant's daughter, and the Commandant's subsequent return from the dead as a statue that invites the unrepentant seducer to a banquet that ends in hell. These supernatural elements were unusual in an age when Greek and Roman literature and mythology inspired most ballets. In the following year Angiolini created the dances for Gluck's opera *Orpheus and Eurydice*, which broke new ground for opera through its insistence on the primacy of drama. Angiolini succeeded Hilverding in St Petersburg as he had in Vienna, making three trips to Russia beginning in 1766. Among his works was a ballet celebrating Catherine II's recovery from vaccination for smallpox. He also composed the music for many of his ballets, and like Hilverding made some attempt to introduce Russian themes, dances and songs into his works.

Although de Hesse, Hilverding and Angiolini each contributed greatly to the evolution of the *ballet d'action*, none of them achieved the lasting renown of Jean Georges Noverre, whose widely disseminated *Letters on Dancing and Ballets*, first published in 1760, exerted a strong influence on choreographers working throughout Europe and fostered public receptivity to the concept of dance drama. Noverre's *Letters* were a vehement call for reform: he wanted choreographers to break with the outmoded formulas of the past in order to create a new type of ballet. He firmly believed that the plot of a good ballet should be constructed logically and rationally, and the action should be intelligible and coherent. Each scene should be consistent in tone, yet the ballet as a whole should display variety and contrast. He disliked the abstractions and symbols that had dominated the court ballet, preferring instead truth to nature (which he qualified, however, as 'beautiful nature'). Although he used mythological figures in his ballets, they had to be motivated by human emotions.

Although some of his ideas may seem self-evident today, he wrote at a time when there was a real need for change. It was common practice in his day for the choreographer, composer, set and costume designers and machinist to work without consulting one another until late in the production process; he called for a closer collaboration and more communication between a ballet's creators. He protested against the use of masks, for he believed that a dancer's

21,22 *Louis René Boquet's costume sketch for Gaetan Vestris as Plaisir in an unidentified ballet depicts the* tonnelet *or short hoop skirt that was the conventional male costume at the Paris Opéra. The choreographer Noverre* (right)*, who became chief balletmaster at the Opéra in 1776, campaigned vigorously against the* tonnelet *and eventually succeeded in having it abolished.*

facial expressions reinforced his gestures and heightened the effect of the emotion he was trying to communicate to the audience. The cumbersome costumes of the period – the women's panniers and the men's *tonnelets* or abbreviated hoop-skirts – also drew his criticism, and he suggested instead that dancers be dressed in light fabrics that moved well and revealed their figures flatteringly. Throughout his *Letters* Noverre recommends that the choreographer study painting, for he must learn to compose stage pictures as a painter does, infusing them with life and expression. He advocated a wide-ranging education for the choreographer, including the observation of people in all walks of life, in order to give greater verisimilitude to stage gesture.

Although Noverre aspired to a post at the Paris Opéra almost from the start of his career, the Opéra's rigid seniority system forced him to spend his formative years working for provincial, foreign and lesser Parisian theatres. In 1755 he was engaged by the English actor-manager David Garrick to mount ballets at Drury Lane, and although this enterprise suffered from the anti-French feeling that eventually led to the Seven Years' War, he profited immensely from his exposure to Garrick's realistic acting style.

Between 1760 and 1767 he spent several highly productive years in Stuttgart, where he had been engaged by the Duke of Wurttemberg, an extremely generous and indulgent patron. *Médée et Jason*, the most popular and frequently revived of his works, was first staged there in 1763 as part of the duke's birthday festivities. It fully justified Noverre's conviction that dance was capable of conveying the strong passions of classical tragedy. Medea, the heroine, is the quintessential woman scorned: she takes her revenge on Jason, the man who has repudiated her, by murdering her children by him, poisoning his new bride and inciting him to stab himself. Noverre's pupil Nancy Levier played Medea opposite the Jason of Gaetan Vestris (1728–1808), a star of the Paris Opéra who was acclaimed as a dancer in the noble style, but nevertheless made annual visits to Stuttgart to dance in the dramatic roles Noverre created for him. In later years Vestris led the way in carrying out one of Noverre's reforms by discarding his mask in the 1770 revival of *Médée et Jason* at the Paris Opéra.

The Stuttgart engagement was followed by an appointment to the court theatres of Vienna, where Noverre found an ensemble of dancers already well versed in dance drama by his predecessors Hilverding and Angiolini. There he staged several tragic ballets, among them his own version of *Les Horaces* (1774), and acquired an important patron in Marie Antoinette, to whom he gave dancing lessons. Thanks to her influence, he was able in 1776 to realize his ambition of becoming the chief balletmaster of the Paris Opéra.

Like many people who have achieved their dreams after long striving, Noverre soon experienced a bitter awakening. He had been appointed over

24 *An Astrologer in the* Ballet du Sérieux et du Grotesque, *presented at the court of Louis XIII in 1627, wears the signs of the zodiac draped about his person: Sagittarius on his head, Cancer and Aries on his left arm, Pisces on his left hip, and so forth.*

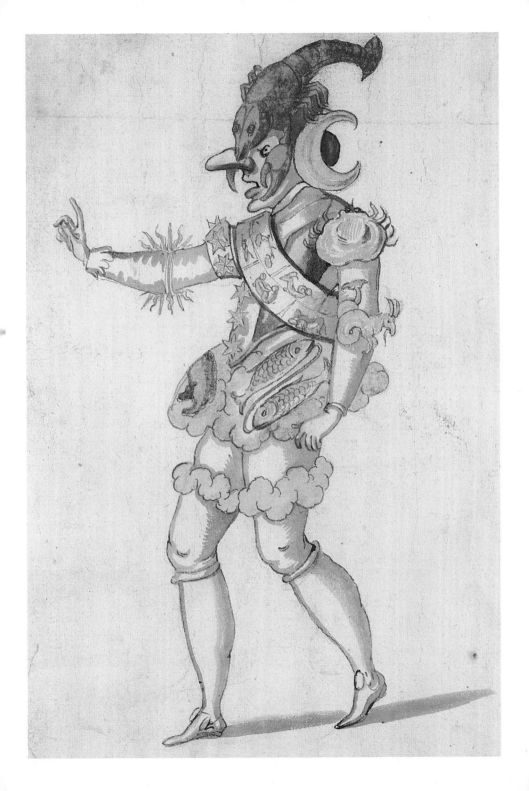

the head of Maximilien Gardel, thus incurring the rancour of the powerful Gardel clan and several of the company's leading dancers. The management of the Opéra also proved to be unsympathetic to his views, ruthlessly using its right to reject his proposals for new ballets. Despite his tribulations Noverre revived a number of his major works for the Opéra, including *Les Horaces*, which may have inspired Jacques Louis David's seminal painting *The Oath of the Horatii*, and *Médée et Jason*. The public, however, considered these ballets too long and complicated, with too little dancing to please them. They preferred works such as *Les Petits Riens* (1778), a lightweight piece on the subject of love and dalliance that Noverre choreographed to a score commissioned from Mozart. Noverre's vicissitudes at the Opéra finally led to his resignation in 1781; however, this was not the end of his career. He returned to England for several successful seasons prior to his retirement in 1797.

He was succeeded at the Opéra by his former pupil Jean Dauberval (1742–1806) and Maximilien Gardel (1741–87), who ruled as joint balletmasters. Dauberval soon left to take up a post at the Grand Theatre of Bordeaux, where he staged his most famous ballet, *La Fille mal gardée* (1789). Although

25, 26 Mozart's Les Petits Riens *(1778) was one of Noverre's great successes at the Paris Opéra; this design for a bergère galante (left) shows the typical costume of the period, with corsets, hooped skirt and high-heeled shoes. In 1787, six years after Noverre had resigned, Pierre Gardel (right) became chief balletmaster at the Opéra, where he stayed until 1820. In later years his conservatism gave the Opéra a name for staidness.*

this ballet appeared on the eve of the French Revolution, its peasant characters and theme (a girl rejects the marriage arranged by her mother, and through a series of lucky coincidences wins her approval to marry the man of her choice) were not treated in a particularly revolutionary manner; unlike Beaumarchais's play *The Marriage of Figaro*, it did not attempt to point out social injustices or call for reform. Dauberval, however, portrayed the lower orders with warmth and sympathy, and though his characters were not entirely realistic, audiences of the time found them more lively and convincing than the porcelain shepherds and shepherdesses who had previously been depicted in pastoral ballets.

During the years of turmoil that followed the French Revolution, the Paris Opéra was kept together by Pierre Gardel (1758–1840), who had succeeded his brother Maximilien as balletmaster in 1787. Gardel, a fervent supporter of the Revolution, collaborated with the painter David on many of its festivals, notably *L'Offrande de la Liberté* (1792), which involved dancers, singers and horses. It included a mimed performance of the 'Marseillaise', which Gardel conceived as a hymn to the goddess of liberty, whom the people worshipped in her temple.

27, 28 Two leading male dancers of the 18th century: left, Auguste Vestris, Gaetan's son, whose dancing was characterized by exuberant virtuosity (the goose was often incorporated in English portraits of him, as a pun on his first name); right, Salvatore Viganò, Italy's leading exponent of the ballet d'action or coreodramma, shown here partnering his wife, Maria Medina. Their light costumes and flat shoes were recent innovations.

In addition to these patriotic offerings, Gardel also produced ballets based on mythological themes, notably *Télémaque* and *Psyché* in 1790 and *Le Jugement de Pâris* in 1793. Like many other choreographers of the period, Gardel had profited from the strictures of Noverre, and his ballets achieved a fine balance between mime and dance passages. His principal dancers included his wife Marie Gardel and Gaetan Vestris's son Auguste (1760–1842), who united brilliant dance technique with considerable acting ability.

Both male and female dancers of this period benefited from the lighter theatrical costumes that had come into fashion. The panniers and *tonnelets* that Noverre had railed against were replaced by flowing, diaphanous dresses in the neoclassical style (which was also in vogue off stage) for the women, and tunics, knee-breeches and stockings for the men. The heeled shoes of the earlier part of the century gave way to sandals or flat-heeled slippers.

Gardel ruled the Paris Opéra virtually singlehandedly until 1820, maintaining firm discipline over the dancers and keeping them in a type of artistic isolation, for he was convinced that Paris was the centre of the ballet world. As a result, choreographers of a more experimental bent were forced to find other outlets for their ideas.

Outside Paris, the development of the *ballet d'action* was carried on by Salvatore Viganò (1769–1821), who had danced in Dauberval's ballets. The first production of his ballet *The Creatures of Prometheus* (Vienna, 1801) is best known today because its score was commissioned from Beethoven, but its expanded version, *Prometeo*, staged in Milan in 1813, was actually more characteristic of the large-scale, spectacular style that he evolved. The ballet's original two acts were lengthened into six, with additional music by Mozart, Haydn and Viganò himself; the story of Prometheus, who created men and gave them fire, was extended to include his punishment and eventual pardon.

Viganò, a highly educated, cultivated man, was not afraid to tackle subjects of broad scope. *Gli Strelizzi*, which he mounted in Venice in 1809, was based upon an actual historical incident: the conspiracy of the Streletz, a troop of armed guards, against Czar Peter I of Russia. Enormous crowd scenes – the ballet included some two hundred supporting characters – contrasted with more intimate moments such as the pas de deux of Peter and his mistress Elizabeth. Viganò choreographed a key scene, the meeting of the conspirators, by giving each performer an individual motivation, which had to be maintained yet coordinated with the group. Viganò's most important work was done at La Scala in Milan between 1812 and 1821. There he collaborated with Alessandro Sanquirico, whose set designs indicate the breadth of Viganò's ballets. Viganò's conception of the *ballet d'action*, which the Italians called *coreodramma*, laid somewhat more stress on acting and mime and less on set dances than its French counterparts.

29 A scene from the English Bach Festival's reconstruction of Jean-Philippe Rameau's comic opéra-ballet Platée *(1745). The plot concerns Jupiter's attempt to disarm Juno's jealousy by feigning love for the ugly river-goddess Platée, seen here with her retinue of frogs.*

Although the 18th century did not solve all the problems of the dramatic ballet, it had certainly taken great strides forward. Ballet had established itself as a legitimate vehicle for dramatic expression, and not merely a decorative adjunct to an opera or play. When the century ended, choreographers were still in the process of exploring the types of themes best handled through movement, but the range of topics that had been successfully treated – mythological tales, classical tragedies, historical dramas, love stories, pastorals and so on – showed that ballet was an art of considerable flexibility. These researches were to be carried further in the 19th century.

30 *Jules Perrot's* Pas de Quatre *(1845) was a showcase for four jewels of the Romantic ballet: (left to right) Carlotta Grisi, Marie Taglioni, Lucile Grahn and Fanny Cerrito.*

CHAPTER FOUR

Ascent and Descent

Ballet achieved its modern identity during the 19th century, or at least acquired many of the characteristics that are now equated with it in the public mind: the pointe technique, or dancing on the tips of the toes; the bouffant skirt called the tutu; the desire to create an illusion of weightlessness and effortlessness; and the association of the female dancer with ethereal creatures of fantasy, such as sylphs and fairies. Significantly, most of these characteristics apply solely to the female dancer, for in the course of the century the male dancer suffered a crushing loss of prestige.

Romanticism was perhaps the most important single influence on 19th-century ballet, though it came later to the ballet than to literature, music or the visual arts. In fact, the Romantic ballet often found inspiration in the works of other Romantic artists; literature was particularly influential and provided themes for many ballets. Despite the diversity of the Romantic movement, the Romantic ballet confined itself principally to two major strands. One was the predilection for the mystical and irrational which appears in Henry Fuseli's paintings, E. T. A. Hoffmann's tales, and programmatic music such as Hector Berlioz's *Symphonie fantastique*. This was manifested in the ballet by themes dealing with supernatural, usually feminine, creatures: sylphides, water nymphs, fire spirits, peris, demons and the like. The allure that such creatures exercised over mortals – as they do in old tales, going back at least as far as the *Odyssey* – became, in the Romantic ballet, a metaphor for the artist's yearning for the unattainable.

A second major preoccupation of the Romantic ballet was the attraction to exotic locales, whether removed in time or space. Similar promptings had led Lord Byron to Greece and Eugène Delacroix to North Africa, while likeminded 19th-century tourists feasted their eyes on the more accessible glories of Italy and the Alps. The passionate interest in history that had led to the Gothic revival in architecture and to what was known in France as the 'troubadour style' in painting and sculpture was reflected in the quasi-medieval settings of many Romantic ballets.

Although the Romantic ballet was, in a sense, a derivative movement, it did not appear overnight, but took time to grow and develop. Many of its characteristics were prefigured by developments in late 18th-century and early 19th-century ballet. The adoption of the soft, close-fitting slipper in the

31, 32 La Sylphide (1832) was the first masterpiece of the Romantic ballet. In this lithograph (left) Marie Taglioni, who danced the leading role in the first production, fetches a bird's nest for her lover. The version choreographed in 1836 by August Bournonville has been lovingly preserved by the Royal Danish Ballet (above).

late 18th century paved the way for the ballerina's rise to the tips of her toes. Choreographers began to introduce elements later associated with the Romantic ballet: Viganò's *Il Noce di Benevento* (Milan, 1812) opened with a witches' sabbath; Gaetano Gioja's *Gabriella di Vergy* (Florence, 1819) set its horrific tale of love and murder in medieval times; and the heroine of Louis Milon's *Nina, ou la folle par amour* (Paris, 1813) succumbed to madness when her father separated her from her chosen lover.

Many of the works of the choreographer Charles Didelot (1767–1837) *33* anticipated the Romantic style. His ballet *Flore et Zéphire*, first performed in London in 1796 and restaged in many different cities, was widely admired for its use of flying machines, which allowed dancers to rise into the air seemingly of their own volition. The pointe technique, then in an experimental stage, was used by some of the ballerinas who danced the role of Flore, among them Geneviève Gosselin. Didelot also used supernatural

33 Charles Didelot with his wife Mme Rose (left) and Mlle Parisot (right) dance in the ballet Alonzo e Cora *at the King's Theatre in London, 1796. The diaphanous dresses of the two women reflect contemporary fashions, but Mlle Parisot's bare breast is probably an example of artistic licence.*

creatures such as sylphs and witches in some of his ballets, but they generally played supporting roles such as guardians or helpers and were not themselves objects of desire.

Romanticism was rather late in reaching the Paris Opéra, where Gardel's long reign had fostered extreme conservatism. Many of the Romantic movement's new ideas were first put into practice in the more innovative atmosphere of the 'boulevard theatres' of Paris (purveyors of popular entertainments such as melodramas, emphasizing sensationalism and spectacle), where several major choreographers of the period, among them Jean Aumer, Jean Coralli, Jules Perrot and Joseph Mazilier, served their apprenticeships. Coralli, for example, staged a sylphides' ballet as early as 1828 in a melodramatic adaptation of Goethe's *Faust*. The boulevard theatres also pioneered the use of illusionistic effects, which helped draw in an audience avid for excitement.

Perhaps the most important technological invention of the era was gas lighting, introduced in London in 1817, although it did not reach the Paris Opéra until 1822. It allowed a more subtle and varied range of effects than the

34 The fashionably eerie atmosphere of a moonlit cloister lined with tombs thrilled the viewers of the ballet of dead nuns in the opera Robert le Diable *(1831). Marie Taglioni, on the brink of stardom, led the spectral revels.*

oil lamps it replaced. The illusion of moonlight that became so important to the Romantic ballet would have been far less convincing without gas lighting.

The immediate impetus for the Romantic ballet is usually credited to a single work, Filippo Taglioni's *La Sylphide*, first produced at the Paris Opéra on 12 March 1832, with Filippo's daughter Marie (1804–84) in the title role. This ballet was such a perfect expression of Romantic urgings that it immediately changed the face of the ballet of its time. Style and subject matter were united in it with a felicitousness that comes rarely to any art form.

31,32

The scenario of *La Sylphide* was written by the tenor Adolphe Nourrit, who had played opposite Marie Taglioni in Giacomo Meyerbeer's opera *Robert le Diable* in the previous year. Marie had danced the leading role in the opera's ghostly ballet of dead nuns, choreographed by her father. Although Nourrit wrote the scenario while the opera was still being rehearsed, he may have been influenced by this scene, which took place in the mysterious moonlit atmosphere of a ruined cloister. His principal inspiration, however,

was Charles Nodier's story *Trilby, ou le Lutin de Argaïl* (1822), in which a male sylph attempts to entice a Scottish peasant girl away from her husband.

Set in Scotland (a locale that had been made both exotic and fashionable by Sir Walter Scott's novels), *La Sylphide* told the story of James Reuben, a discontented young man who abandons the mundane world – and his mortal fiancée – in order to pursue an alluring otherworldly creature, the Sylphide. He follows her to her own habitat, a wild and tenebrous forest, but she eludes all his attempts to detain her. In desperation he seeks the help of a witch (the horrific aspect of the otherworld), who gives him an enchanted scarf that will bind the Sylphide to him. But the scarf proves to be fatal to the Sylphide, whose body is borne away through the treetops by her sister sylphides.

Although the ballet might be interpreted as a cautionary tale – for James sees the wedding procession of his fiancée and his rival as the ballet ends – the Sylphide was characterized as such an appealing figure that the audience could not help but sympathize with James's attraction to her. Marie Taglioni's dancing was in large part responsible for this, for she infused the role with such poetry that dancers and nondancers alike strove to imitate her, the former by learning to dance on their toes or 'taglioniser', and the latter by donning apparel and coiffures 'à la Sylphide'. Taglioni's performance demonstrated the expressive potential of the pointe technique, which had previously been used principally as an acrobatic feat by most of its early practitioners, such as the Italian ballerina Amalia Brugnoli. Equally important were Taglioni's effortlessness, lightness and fluidity of movement, which, coupled with her chaste and modest bearing, made her appear to be indeed an airy being innocent of human lusts and desires.

La Sylphide created a rage for a new type of heroine, derived from the ethereal creatures of folklore rather than the goddesses, shepherdesses and nymphs of the antique world. These beings were almost always costumed in a variant of the Sylphide's bell-shaped skirt, adapted from the ball dresses of the period and made of many layers of diaphanous muslin, which later became known by its French slang name, 'tutu'. The popularity of this costume gave the name of 'ballet blanc' or 'white ballet' to the new genre.

Taglioni's reign was unchallenged until 1834, when the Viennese ballerina Fanny Elssler (1810–84) was engaged by the Paris Opéra. Elssler's style of dancing was very different from Taglioni's, for her special gift lay in the precision and rapidity with which she executed small, quick steps. Her type of dancing was called *danse tacquetée* to distinguish it from the airborne *danse ballonné*, characterized by leaps and jumps of an ineffable lightness, in which Taglioni excelled. Although the Opéra's management had deliberately selected Elssler as a foil to Taglioni, she did not find an equivalent to Taglioni's role of the Sylphide until 1836, when she first performed the

35 Fanny Elssler's vivacious Cachucha ravished audiences throughout Europe and America. This lithograph depicts Jean-Auguste Barre's bronze statuette of the dancer, which was exhibited in the Paris Salon of 1837.

Cachucha, a balleticized Spanish dance, in Coralli's ballet *Le Diable boiteux*. Spanish dancers were much in vogue throughout the 19th century in Paris, London and other European cities; among them was Lola de Valence, whom Edouard Manet painted in the 1860s. Although Elssler was not Spanish, audiences did not cavil at her *Cachucha*, which she danced with such fire and sensuous vitality that the poet Théophile Gautier dubbed her the 'pagan' dancer, in contrast to Taglioni, the 'Christian' dancer. Like Camargo and Sallé in an earlier era, Taglioni and Elssler came to represent two different but complementary aspects of the art of ballet, and their images were often juxtaposed in the roles most closely identified with them: Taglioni in white muslin as the ethereal Sylphide, Elssler in pink satin and black lace as the voluptuous Spanish dancer.

Elssler's success in the *Cachucha* led to a craze for balleticized national dances of all kinds. Not surprisingly, Elssler herself was the major exponent of this type of dancing, and soon added to her repertory a Polish cracovienne, an Italian tarantella, and others. The folk dances of Europe – and occasionally of other continents – were plundered enthusiastically by ballet choreographers and dancers in search of local colour.

In addition to her technical gifts, Elssler also possessed an exceptional degree of dramatic ability, and her performances of the great roles of the Romantic ballet illuminated new aspects of the characters. She invested Taglioni's role of the Sylphide with a heightened sense of drama, and gave strong and convincing interpretations of the roles of Giselle and Esmeralda, although neither was created for her.

Giselle (1841), the only ballet of the Romantic period that has survived in continuous performance to this day, was created for the third great ballerina of the period, Carlotta Grisi (1819–99). The choreography of this ballet was divided between Coralli, the chief balletmaster at the Paris Opéra, who arranged its ensemble dances, and Jules Perrot (1810–92), Grisi's mentor and common-law husband, who created Grisi's dances. Perrot himself was a gifted dancer whose elevation had earned him the nickname 'the aerial'. The choreography of *Giselle* brought out a new facet of his genius.

Giselle combined the elements of local colour and supernaturalism with compelling dramatic logic. It was conceived by Gautier, who found his inspiration in the descriptions of German folklore in Heinrich Heine's *De l'Allemagne*. Gautier was fascinated by Heine's account of the wilis, nocturnal feminine spirits who forced men to dance until they died of exhaustion. The role of Giselle allowed the ballerina to inhabit both of the Romantic ballet's favourite worlds. In the first act, set in a medieval village on the Rhine, she is a peasant girl in love with the nobleman Albrecht, who is disguised as a peasant. The revelation of his true identity and his engagement to a woman of his own rank catapults her into madness, and she commits suicide with his sword (or, in some productions, dies of a broken heart). In the second act she reappears as a wili, but unlike her bloodthirsty sisters she has no desire to revenge herself upon her repentant lover. Her undying love protects him until dawn breaks the wilis' malevolent power.

The score of *Giselle*, composed by Adolphe Adam, was notable for its use of leitmotives, which were then a rarity in ballet music. Adam used this device with telling effect in Giselle's mad scene, when the themes that had accompanied her first carefree dances with Albrecht recur as she relives her memories of former happiness. The score was also unusual for its period in being almost totally original instead of an assemblage of borrowed melodies.

Despite Perrot's hopes, the success of *Giselle* did not secure him a permanent position at the Opéra, and therefore his major choreography of the 1840s was done in London rather than Paris. His best dramatic ballets were notable for their use of dance movement to advance the action, for most ballets of the period communicated their plots through a stylized form of mime. In *Ondine* (1843), which was loosely based on a story by Friedrich de la Motte Fouqué, Perrot graphically depicted the dangers of the supernatural

36, 37 Giselle was created in 1841 for the great ballerina Carlotta Grisi (left); the libretto was written by her devoted admirer Théophile Gautier. Grisi lived with the dancer Jules Perrot, who helped to choreograph the ballet; on the right they are shown dancing the polka, which they did much to popularize.

world by making the water nymph Ondine lure her would-be lover Matteo to the brink of a precipice, from which she blithely leaps into her own native element, the sea. Later she dances with her newly discovered shadow, having assumed mortal substance in order to marry Matteo.

La Esmeralda (1844), one of Perrot's most successful dramatic ballets, was derived from Victor Hugo's *Notre Dame de Paris* (1831). It was created in London with Grisi in the title role and later restaged with great success in Milan and St Petersburg, though never in Paris. Set in the Middle Ages, a period dear to the hearts of many Romantic painters and writers, *La Esmeralda* changed the focus of Hugo's novel by concentrating on the vicissitudes of the gypsy dancing girl Esmeralda. In addition, Perrot changed the ending to a happy one in which Esmeralda, who has been falsely accused of murder, is vindicated and wins the hand of the man she loves, the aristocratic Phoebus de Chateaupers.

Perrot also developed a contrasting type of ballet that focused above all on the dancing (as opposed to acting) skills of its performers. The first of this

38 In a period when the male dancer was an endangered species, Arthur Saint-Léon (centre) was one of the few to win approval. In Jules Perrot's La Esmeralda *(1844), Fleur-de-Lys (Adelaide Frassi, left) and the gypsy Esmeralda (Carlotta Grisi, with tambourine) vied for his love.*

30 genre was the *Pas de Quatre* of 1845, which united Taglioni, Grisi, Fanny Cerrito and Lucile Grahn in a divertissement (a series of plotless dances) that displayed the particular gifts of each ballerina. Some of his later ballets of this type were held together by a slender thread of plot: in *The Judgment of Paris* (1846), Taglioni, Cerrito and Grahn were goddesses who vied for the approval of the shepherd Paris, played by Arthur Saint-Léon, one of the few male dancers of the period to win the favour of a public besotted by ballerinas. Although the Romantic period did not lack good male dancers, Perrot and Saint-Léon foremost among them, ballets such as the *Pas de Quatre* confirmed the public in its overriding adulation of the ballerina. As the male dancer's status and morale declined, fewer men entered the profession, until in the latter part of the century male dancers were practically reduced to stage decoration, and women in travesty played the leading male roles.

Perrot's work in London was part of the international expansion of the Romantic ballet, a process to which both dancers and choreographers contributed. Most of the great ballerinas of the period were widely travelled, being much in demand in the cultural centres of Europe, where they danced the famous roles of their repertories. Taglioni and Elssler both made the arduous journey to Russia to dance in St Petersburg and Moscow. Taglioni first went there in 1837, accompanied by her father, who staged several new ballets for her there. *La Gitana* (1838), the most famous of these, presented her with the challenge of performing a dance similar to Elssler's *Cachucha*, but she acquitted herself well enough to win considerable success.

Elssler's travels took her to the west as well as to the east; from 1840 until 1842 she toured the United States and Cuba. She was not the only European dancer to seek fame and fortune in America, having been preceded by lesser lights such as Celeste Keppler, known by the single name of Celeste, who performed in many staples of the European Romantic repertory; and Paul and Amalia Taglioni (the brother and sister-in-law of Marie), who presented the first complete and authentic version of *La Sylphide* in America in 1839. Elssler, however, was certainly the greatest dancer of the period to cross the Atlantic, and her appearances created the type of sensation that is more commonly associated today with film and rock stars. Among her admirers were the authors Ralph Waldo Emerson and Henry Wadsworth Longfellow.

In Europe, choreographers such as Perrot were often engaged as guests by the opera houses of various cities. They restaged their most famous works and often created new ones as well. Alternatively, a resident choreographer might stage his own versions of the famous ballets of the period, altering and

39 August Bournonville's ballets brought a taste of Romanticism to Denmark. In this contemporary lithograph, Junker Ove, the hero of A Folk Tale *(1854), is surrounded by a bevy of dangerously alluring elf-maidens.*

occasionally improving them in the process. In Milan the choreographer Antonio Cortesi staged an expanded version of *Giselle* in 1843, adding to the cast a saintly old hermit who helps the heroine, and an apotheosis set in the kingdom of the wilis.

Although more has been published to date about ballet in Paris and London than in other European cities, a great deal of activity took place outside these two centres. In Copenhagen, the Romantic ballet was imported from Paris by a native son, August Bournonville (1805–79), who studied and danced at the Opéra, then returned to Denmark to become the director of the ballet at the Royal Theatre. One of his best known and most frequently reproduced works was his revision of *La Sylphide*, which he first mounted in 1836 with a new score by a Danish composer, Herman Løvenskjold. He also created many original works as well. In Bournonville's ballets the demonic element of Romanticism is kept under firm control, and its perilous attraction is never allowed to triumph over human values. In *A Folk Tale* (1854), the hero encounters a lovely girl who appears to be a dangerous supernatural creature. However, she proves to be a human changeling who lifts the spell laid upon him by the elf-maidens and ultimately is restored to her true home.

Milan also enjoyed a special prominence in the world of 19th-century ballet. In the early part of the century Carlo Blasis (1795–1878), famed as a teacher and theorist, built up the Imperiale Regia Accademia di Danze into one of the most important schools of the period. The ballerinas trained there were renowned for their dazzling technique, which a few of them, notably Carolina Rosati (1826–1905) and Virginia Zucchi (1849–1930), wedded to considerable dramatic talent. These dancers were soon in demand everywhere in Europe: Rosati went to London, where she danced in Perrot's ballets of the late 1840s; Sofia Fuoco, a dancer known for her pointe work, performed at the Paris Opéra. Zucchi enjoyed a brilliant career in Russia, where she was particularly acclaimed for her moving portrayal of the title role of Perrot's *La Esmeralda*. Pierina Legnani (1863–1923), who made her name through her ability to execute thirty-two consecutive fouettés or whipped turns, took this feat to Russia, where it was incorporated in Marius Petipa's *Swan Lake* (1895) and has served ever since as a test of the ballerina's ability.

The Romantic ballet of the 1830s and 1840s was fashionable and newsworthy, and its influence was pervasive. Satirical cartoons depicted prominent politicians of the day in the guise of rather ungainly ballerinas. Authors such as Charles Dickens and William Makepeace Thackeray alluded to the ballet in their writings: Dickens gives a detailed description of the ballet of the 'Indian Savage and the Maiden' in *Nicholas Nickleby* (1839), while Thackeray's Becky Sharp of *Vanity Fair* (1847), the daughter of a dancer,

40, 41 The Italian ballerina Virginia Zucchi (left) became famous throughout Europe for her beauty and dramatic talent as well as for her virtuoso technical ability. The teenaged Giuseppina Bozzachi (right) played Swanilda in the premiere of Arthur Saint-Léon's Coppélia *(1870). She died tragically early, her promise unfulfilled, in the Franco-Prussian War.*

executes a waltz so well at a ball that 'the company . . . applauded as wildly as if she had been a Noblet or a Taglioni' (the French ballerina Lise Noblet is mentioned repeatedly by Thackeray). Figures of ballerinas are peppered throughout the pages of *Punch*, the *Illustrated London News*, and other British journals. In France Honoré de Balzac included dancers among the wide range of characters represented in his monumental cycle *The Human Comedy*.

As the mid-century approached, however, the Romantic ballet began to lose its impact. More and more, elaborate stage effects began to dominate ballet productions. Theatrical tricks had, of course, been used to good effect in many ballets, among them *Flore et Zéphire* and *La Sylphide*. Occasionally, however, stage spectacle overshadowed the rest of the action on stage: despite a complicated plot superficially based on Byron's poem, Joseph Mazilier's *Le Corsaire* (1856) was notable chiefly for its realistic storm and shipwreck.

The last great choreographer of the 19th century was Arthur Saint-Léon (1821–70), a gifted dancer, choreographer and violinist, and the inventor of a system of dance notation called *sténochorégraphie*. Active in both Russia and

38

western Europe, he tried to enrich the vocabulary of academic ballet with steps and gestures derived from folk dance. His ballet *The Little Humpbacked Horse*, first presented in St Petersburg in 1864, was based upon the exploits of the folk hero Ivanushka, who wins the beautiful Tsar-Maiden as his bride. At the Paris Opéra, Saint-Léon created his best-known ballet, the perennially popular *Coppélia* (1870), to a score by Léo Delibes. Inspired by E. T. A. Hoffmann's *Der Sandmann*, a fantastic tale that Jacques Offenbach also used for the first act of his opera *The Tales of Hoffmann* (1881), *Coppélia* told the story of Swanilda, a girl who takes the place of an automated doll that has infatuated her sweetheart Franz, who believes it to be real. This imposture also deludes the doll's inventor, Dr Coppélius, into believing that his creation has come to life. The ballet's concluding divertissement, which celebrates the wedding of Swanilda and Franz, revealed Saint-Léon's preference for dancing rather than drama, and reflected the growing taste for spectacle.

The Franco-Prussian War broke out shortly after the ballet's premiere, and both Saint-Léon and Giuseppina Bozzacchi, the sixteen-year-old Milanese dancer who had played Swanilda, died before the end of the year. Saint-Léon was succeeded at the Opéra by Louis Mérante, a competent but colourless choreographer. Italian ballerinas dominated the Opéra's stage; the most prominent among them was Carlotta Zambelli (1875–1968), a dancer of great charm and formidable technique. Only one male dancer, Miguel Vasquez, made any mark upon the Opéra at this time.

The ballet of this period was immortalized, however, by the paintings and drawings of Edgar Degas, who painted dancers in class, at rehearsal and in performance. The overwhelming majority of his subjects are female, though a few male teachers and balletmasters – notably Mérante and the ageing Perrot – may be identified among them. With a few exceptions (among them the Ballet of the Nuns in *Robert le Diable*), Degas rarely identified the specific ballets he was depicting, for he was more engaged with his studies of colour, composition and form than with creating a record of the Opéra's performances. Nevertheless, his pictures vividly capture the appearance and atmosphere of the Paris Opéra ballet from the 1860s to 1900.

In the last quarter of the century, the ballet seemed to have abandoned the Romantic period's poetry and expressiveness – its appeal to the heart – in favour of a more superficial concentration on technical virtuosity and visual spectacle. These elements were certainly predominant in the ballets of Luigi Manzotti (1835–1905), which were produced in many European cities, including London and Paris, as well as in his native Milan. *Excelsior* (1881), his most successful ballet, celebrated the great technological achievements of mankind, among them the discovery of electricity, the invention of the telegraph and the appearance of the first steamboat.

42 *19th-century audiences revelled in the pageantry of Luigi Manzotti's
spectacular* Excelsior *(1881), with its huge cast of dancers and supernumeraries
and its opulent sets and costumes. The ballet portrayed the rise of human
civilization as a struggle between the spirits of Light and Darkness.*

By the close of the century, ballet in western Europe had reached a very
low point. The great choreographers of the Romantic era were dead, and no
new talents had risen to take their places. Ballet seemed to have lost its
creative momentum, and the public had ceased to regard it as a serious art
form. It was no longer a mainstream art, as it had been in the 1830s and 1840s;
it had lost touch with the times. Indeed, ballet bore all the symptoms of an art
about to die of exhaustion.

CHAPTER FIVE

Crystallization and Ferment in Russia

'Russian ballet': from the 1910s to the 1930s these words spelled magic to the general public, and even today they evoke visions of theatrical excitement. Russian dancers such as Vaslav Nijinsky and Anna Pavlova have passed into legend, and the association of Russian nationality and genius in dancing has enhanced the very real gifts of present-day dancers such as Rudolf Nureyev, Natalia Makarova and Mikhail Baryshnikov. Indeed, around the 1930s it was widely believed that only Russians had the capacity to become great ballet dancers.

The Russian ballet's renown in the west is, however, a fairly recent phenomenon, dating only from the early 20th century. The history of Russian ballet itself actually goes back much further. Ballet was first introduced at the 17th-century court of Czar Alexei. A professional dancing school was started in 1738 by the Frenchman Jean-Baptiste Landé, and when the Imperial Theatres became a state system in 1756, ballet was included as one of its branches. A long list of foreign guest artists enriched the ballet in St Petersburg and Moscow, Russia's two major cultural centres. Hilverding and Angiolini imported the *ballet d'action* in the 18th century. Didelot, whose ballets prefigured the Romantic period, worked in Russia in the early 19th century. His ballet *The Prisoner of the Caucasus* (1823), inspired by a poem by the Russian poet Alexander Pushkin, incorporated Circassian folk dances, games and contests. During the Romantic era, Taglioni and Elssler danced in Russia, and Perrot and Saint-Léon both performed and choreographed for the Imperial Theatres. Indeed, Saint-Léon took especial pride in his ballet *The Little Humpbacked Horse* (see page 58), which was based on Russian themes.

There was no lack of native-born talent, although before the 20th century Russian dancers and choreographers tended to be overshadowed by their foreign counterparts. Ivan Valberkh (1766–1819), the first Russian choreographer of note, often portrayed ordinary people in realistic surroundings. His ballet *The New Heroine, or the Woman Cossack* (1812) was based on the story of Nadezhda Durova, a real-life heroine of the war against Napoleon. The same patriotic fervour inspired Adam Gluszowski (1793–c.1870) to use Russian folk dances and customs as the basis of much of his choreography. He created the first ballet inspired by Pushkin's poetry, *Ruslan and Ludmilla* (1821).

43 The Spirit of the Rose (Vaslav Nijinsky) gently invades the dreams of a girl (Tamara Karsavina) fresh from her first ball in Michel Fokine's Le Spectre de la Rose *(1911), one of the greatest successes of Diaghilev's Ballets Russes.*

Among the many fine dancers trained by the imperial ballet schools was Avdotia Istomina (1799–1848), who danced the principal female role in Didelot's *The Prisoner of the Caucasus* and was eulogized in Pushkin's poem *Eugene Onegin*. The gifted dancer-actress Yelena Andreyanova (1819–57), the first Russian ballerina to dance the role of Giselle, performed leading roles in the Russian stagings of many Romantic ballets. Nadezdha Bogdanova and Martha Muravieva both danced in Western Europe during the mid-19th century, and were in fact more successful there than in their native country, where they were disadvantaged by the preference for foreign ballerinas.

Until the late 19th century Russia played the role of follower rather than a leader in the world of dance. This situation was reversed, however, within the brief span of the two decades between 1890 and 1910, which marked the apogee of the classical ballet, exemplified by the works of the French-born choreographer Marius Petipa (1818–1910), and the beginning of a new approach to choreography instigated by the Russian Mikhail Fokine (1880–1942), later well-known in the west as Michel Fokine. Petipa's efforts preserved the art of ballet at a high level at a time when it was all but moribund in Western Europe; the reforms urged by Fokine gave it a new vitality. The transition between the two may be seen as the passing of the torch from France, the birthplace of ballet, to Russia, where ballet was renewed.

The term 'classical ballet', which is most often associated with ballets such as *The Sleeping Beauty* and *Swan Lake*, indicates a concept of choreography that stresses formal values such as clarity, harmony, symmetry and order. The academic ballet technique is paramount and its rules are rarely transgressed. Although classical ballets are not entirely devoid of emotional content, this aspect usually takes second place. At its best Petipa's choreography is notable for its high degree of inventiveness and variety; he made the emphasis upon form into a positive attribute, capable of capturing and holding an audience's interest. An extremely prolific choreographer, he often created 'reserve pieces' which could be adapted at need to specific ballets.

The classical ballet's sense of order is demonstrated by the crystallization of the pas de deux, which almost always has a well-defined structure in Petipa's ballets: the opening adagio for the ballerina and her partner is followed by variations (solos) for each dancer. The two dancers again join in the concluding coda, which is usually a display of pyrotechnics. The ballerina is invariably the focal point of the pas de deux, and the male dancer's function is chiefly to support her and display her beauty.

Classical dancing in Petipa's ballets is often contrasted with character dances (balleticized folk or national dances) which add the local colour and exoticism that had become popular in the Romantic era. These dances are rarely authentic. The folk movements are performed with more softness and fluidity than their originals; feet are stretched and arms rounded in accordance with the rules of academic ballet technique.

Petipa arrived in St Petersburg in 1847. Although he was engaged by the Imperial Theatres as a dancer, he already had some experience as a choreographer. In December 1849 Perrot assumed the position of balletmaster in St Petersburg, and Petipa played leading roles in a number of his great dramatic ballets, among them *Esmeralda* and *Faust*, and assisted him in restaging several works. In 1850 he restaged *Giselle* according to Perrot's instructions, reworking the dances of the wilis in the second act. He made a more substantial revision, known as the 'Grand Pas de Wilis', in 1884. In 1859 Saint-Léon assumed Perrot's post at the Imperial Theatres. Unlike Perrot, he emphasized dancing rather than drama; his choreography for soloists was considered particularly good. He often used folk dances as a source of inspiration for steps and movements, and his work showed Petipa the value of variety in choreography.

Petipa's first great success, *Pharaoh's Daughter* (1862), was produced during Saint-Léon's term as balletmaster. It was a fantasy of ancient Egypt, inspired by Gautier's *Le Roman de la Momie*. The role of Aspicia, Pharaoh's daughter, was danced by the Italian ballerina Carolina Rosati, then on the verge of retirement, while the Englishman Lord Wilson was danced by Petipa himself. Under the influence of opium, Lord Wilson dreams that he is an Egyptian youth, Ta-Hor, who rescues Aspicia from a lion and wins her love. Their ultimate union, however, is forestalled by the ending of the dream. In addition to its dramatic scenes, the ballet included many pure dance passages, among them a divertissement by the great rivers of the world. Divertissements of this sort appeared in many of Petipa's ballets, for they gave Russian dancers a chance to display their talents at a time when leading roles were usually assigned to foreign guest artists.

Aspicia's costume, which was typical of its period, consisted of a tutu ornamented with 'Egyptian' devices, worn with a contemporary hairstyle and jewellery. The tutu, which had been shortened since Taglioni's day, had become the ballerina's uniform and the mark of her status; it was worn regardless of country and period, with minor changes in its decoration to suggest national or period character. This practice later became one of the targets of Fokine's programme of reform. In contrast, the corps de ballet was usually dressed in more authentic period costume, and the sets generally revealed considerable research.

Petipa's *La Bayadère* (1877), based on the play *Sakuntala* by the Indian poet Kalidasa, had as its heroine a temple dancer, Nikiya, who loses her lover Solor to the daughter of a rajah. Character dances such as the 'Hindu Dance', inspired by the Indian dance form called Kathak, were juxtaposed with classical sequences such as the fourth-act 'Kingdom of the Shades', in which Solor has an opium-induced vision of Nikiya, murdered by her rival in the preceding act. This scene takes place in a sphere far removed from the real world; in contrast to the local colour and emotional tension of the earlier acts, the dancers in their identical white tutus radiate a serene detachment. Although Solor sees himself dancing with Nikiya, she is no more than a projection of his own remorse and yearning. In terms of dramatic action, nothing happens in this scene, yet its choreography and music speak so powerfully to the viewer that it has preserved its freshness while the ballet's dramatic scenes have come to appear dated.

In the 1880s ballet in Russia began to enjoy a surge in popularity, thanks to the appearances of the Italian ballerina Virginia Zucchi, whose exceptional dramatic gifts were compared to those of the actresses Sarah Bernhardt and Eleonora Duse. She excelled in intensely dramatic ballets such as *Esmeralda* and Hippolyte Monplaisir's *Brahma*, the story of a slave girl who becomes the lover of the Hindu god Brahma during his sojourn on earth. Yet she was also a skillful comedienne, capable of enchanting audiences in lighter works such as *La Fille mal gardée* and *Coppélia*. She inspired a passion for ballet in many individuals who helped shape Russian ballet in the late 19th and early 20th centuries, among them the young artist Alexandre Benois (1870–1960), who became a key figure in the formation of Serge Diaghilev's Ballets Russes.

Ivan Vsevolojsky, the director of the Imperial Theatres, decided to capitalize upon the public's interest in ballet by commissioning a ballet score from Peter Ilyich Tchaikovsky, who had already gained some fame as a composer. Vsevolojsky selected the story of *The Sleeping Beauty*, which he conceived as a sumptuous tribute to the period of Louis XIV. In describing his intentions to Tchaikovsky, he invoked the names of Rameau and Lully. At this time most ballet scores were composed by poorly esteemed specialists, who customarily followed explicit instructions supplied by the choreographer. Petipa accordingly gave Tchaikovsky a detailed scenario, indicating tempi, duration and atmosphere for each scene. But Tchaikovsky transcended Petipa's scenario, investing the score with a quality akin to that of symphonic music.

The plot of *The Sleeping Beauty*, first performed in 1890, was adapted from Charles Perrault's well-known fairy tale. In the ballet, it became the pretext for some of Petipa's finest choreography, dances that exalt the academic ballet technique. The ballet alternates mime scenes, dances expressive of emotion and dances that celebrate dancing for the sake of dancing. Their number and variety gave each member of the company an opportunity to shine. The ballet's prologue, which depicts Princess Aurora's christening,

40

44 Marius Petipa created a number of gem-like solos for The Sleeping Beauty *(1890), among them the dance of the fairy Fleur de Farine (wheat flour), danced by Marie Anderson (centre). The abstract quality of these dances has allowed their names to be changed freely, and other companies have renamed this solo Cherry Blossom, Enchanted Gardens, Honour or Generosity.*

contains a variation for each of the six fairies who have come to bestow gifts upon the infant. The prologue ends with the confrontation of the wicked fairy Carabosse, who places a curse upon Aurora, and the good Lilac Fairy, who mitigates the curse from death to sleep.

The choreographic high point of the first act, which takes place on Aurora's sixteenth birthday, is the 'Rose Adagio' that she dances with four suitors, revealing a young girl's growing confidence through the triumphant balances in attitude (a pose similar to an arabesque, but with a bent knee) that crown the dance. This act too ends dramatically, as Aurora pricks her finger and falls into her hundred-years' sleep. In the 'Vision Scene' of the second act, the Lilac Fairy shows the hero, Prince Désiré, an enticing apparition of Aurora, but the female ensemble, dancing between them, prevents him from making more than fleeting contact with her. By the final act of the ballet Aurora has been awakened and all dramatic tension has been resolved. The couple's wedding is celebrated with a divertissement by various fairy tale characters, among them Puss in Boots, Little Red Riding Hood and the Blue Bird. In the grand pas de deux, Aurora is presented as a woman in full bloom, rejoicing in true love.

Overleaf 45 Present-day choreographers have attempted a number of new interpretations of Lev Ivanov's The Nutcracker, *often bringing out horrific or erotic elements of its fantasies. The genial partygoers in Rudolf Nureyev's version, first mounted in 1967, later appear as terrifying bats in the heroine's nightmare.*

95

The role of Aurora was danced by the Italian ballerina Carlotta Brianza. Prince Désiré was danced by Pavel Gerdt, the leading male dancer of the Russian stage and an exemplar of manly elegance and nobility. Another Italian dancer, Enrico Cecchetti, doubled the roles of Carabosse (in travesty) and the Blue Bird. Petipa's daughter Marie played the Lilac Fairy, which was then primarily a mime role.

The Sleeping Beauty won the public's favour, and Vsevolojsky deemed it enough of a success to commission Tchaikovsky to compose the score for a second ballet, *The Nutcracker* (1892), based upon Alexandre Dumas père's adaptation of Hoffmann's fantastic tale *Nutcracker and Mouse King*. Most of the dramatic interest was concentrated in the first act, in which little Clara helps the nutcracker (who is really an enchanted prince) to win a battle against the mice and is invited to accompany him to the Kingdom of Sweets. The second act consisted of an extended divertissement by the subjects of the Sugarplum Fairy, who was danced by an Italian guest artist, Antonietta dell'Era. Petipa fell ill before he could begin work on the ballet, and it was entrusted to Lev Ivanov (1834–1901), his assistant. Ivanov, who had created the role of Solor in *La Bayadère*, had an unusual gift for music, including a memory that allowed him to perform compositions after a single hearing. His best work achieved what has been called a symphonic quality in dance, expressing emotion through pure classical dancing without an explicit plotline or pantomime. The most successful of his dances for *The Nutcracker*, 'The Waltz of the Snowflakes', marked the passage of Clara and her prince through a snowy landscape; its choreography, which evoked the movements of windswept snow, was so admired that connoisseurs sat in the upper tiers of the theatre the better to watch its myriad patterns.

In 1895 Ivanov and Petipa collaborated on *Swan Lake*, the third of Tchaikovsky's great ballet scores. This ballet had been produced in Moscow in 1877, but had achieved only a limited success because of the weakness of the choreography by Julius Wenzel Reisinger. The 1895 production, mounted after Tchaikovsky's death, incorporated certain changes in the scenario and score, which were arranged with the help of the composer's brother Modeste. Based on the widespread folkloric theme of maidens who have been magically transformed into swans, the ballet depicted the doomed love of Prince Siegfried and the swan queen Odette. The evil magician Rothbart, whose sorcery binds Odette, tricks Siegfried into breaking his vow of fidelity to Odette by introducing an imposter, Odile (usually played by the same ballerina who dances Odette). The spell is broken, however, when Siegfried sacrifices himself for Odette, with whom he is reunited in death.

The first and third acts of the ballet, set at the court ruled by Siegfried and his mother, were choreographed by Petipa, while Ivanov was responsible for the more magical second and fourth acts, set beside the lake where Odette and her fellow swan-maidens nightly resume their human forms. Though Petipa's dances were varied and colourful, particularly the character dances of the third-act ballroom scene, Ivanov's masterly deployment of the ensemble of swan-maidens more closely captured the impassioned sweep of Tchaikovsky's music. In the second act duet for Odette and Siegfried, familiarly known as the 'White Swan' pas de deux, he broke with the set form of the pas de deux established by Petipa and choreographed instead a single prolonged adagio.

The poetic 'White Swan' contrasts sharply with Petipa's 'Black Swan' pas de deux of the third act, in which the glamorous Odile, symbolically dressed in a black tutu, dazzles Siegfried with a display of virtuosity. Here Petipa employed to good effect the thirty-two consecutive fouettés (whipped turns) that were the speciality of his leading ballerina, Pierina Legnani, lending a sense of dramatic motivation to a feat that hovered dangerously close to a circus trick. Although the choreography of the 'Black Swan' pas de deux was closer in style to her Italian training, Legnani also acquitted herself well in the subtler role of Odette. The dual role of Odette/Odile remains one of the most coveted and challenging roles of the classical repertory.

46 In the St Petersburg premiere of Swan Lake (1895), the role of Prince Siegfried was played by the fifty-year-old Pavel Gerdt (right), necessitating the addition of the role of Benno, the prince's friend, to provide actual support for the ballerina.

Left 47 *The stage and costume designs that Léon Bakst created for
Schéhérazade (1910) sparked new fashions in the worlds of dress design and
interior decoration. His use of strong, jewel-like colours was particularly
imitated: the combination of green and blue in this detail of his design for the
backdrop is especially characteristic.*

Above 48 *Bakst's design for Nijinsky's costume in* L'Après-midi d'un faune
(1912) evokes the languid, dream-like quality of the ballet.

These three ballets to Tchaikovsky's music – *The Sleeping Beauty*, *The Nutcracker* and *Swan Lake* – have enjoyed continuing success on the ballet stage. Innumerable dancers have made their names in one or another of the great roles they offer, and many more have received valuable performing experience in lesser roles. *The Nutcracker*, which has become a Christmas-time institution in numerous cities, offers many children their first opportunity to dance on stage.

Despite Petipa and Ivanov's demonstration of the power and capacity of the classical ballet, the early 20th century saw a turn away from formalism in Russian ballet. Alexander Gorsky (1871–1924), who did his most significant work in Moscow, was strongly influenced by Konstantin Stanislavsky's Art Theatre of Moscow, which aimed at creating a form of drama that would be more true to nature. Gorsky attempted to translate Stanislavsky's principles to the ballet: in his version of *Don Quixote* (1900), he furnished each member of the ensemble with a task and motivation. Like Perrot's *Esmeralda*, Gorsky's *Gudule's Daughter* (1902) was derived from Hugo's *Notre Dame de Paris*, but Gorsky scorned Perrot's use of a happy ending. His Esmeralda, like Hugo's, did not escape execution for the crime of which she had been unjustly accused: the ballet's powerful ending depicted her slow progress to the scaffold, her last-minute reunion with her long-lost mother Gudule and the crowd's frantic attempts to rescue her.

Gorsky's experiments foreshadowed the work of Michel Fokine, who had graduated from the Imperial Ballet School in 1898. He attacked the ballet's blind conformity to tradition, such as its dependence upon a highly stylized and artificial form of mime that was meaningless to most of the audience, and the ballerina's inevitable costume of tutu and pointe shoes. Although he did not advocate the complete abandonment of academic ballet technique, which he considered the only form of training that could equip a dancer with the necessary strength and versatility, he believed that the choreographer should be able to dispense with it if the ballet's theme so required. He considered pointe work inappropriate to many themes, and replaced it with his own conceptions of various period and national dance forms.

Fokine saw Isadora Duncan dance during her first trip to Russia in 1904 (see page 90), and although in later life he denied having been influenced by her, she may have stimulated him to experiment with a freer use of the arms and torso. Most of his early choreography was produced for student or charity performances. His first full-length ballet, *Acis and Galatea*, presented at a student performance in 1905, shared the Greek inspiration that is associated with Duncan's dancing; it also applied his pet theory of devising a new movement style to suit each ballet, for he used tumbling instead of academic ballet technique in a fauns' dance. Among the boys who played the fauns was

49 Les Sylphides *(1909), arguably Fokine's most popular ballet, has been performed by ballet companies all over the world. Its fluid movements of the arms and upper torso are sometimes attributed to the influence of Isadora Duncan. Karsavina is the standing figure in front of the group at right.*

Vaslav Nijinsky, whose extraordinary elevation had already been noticed by his teachers.

Fokine carried his technical and costume reforms further in *Eunice* (1907). Basing his choreography on his study of Greek vase-painting and Egyptian sculpture, he avoided virtuosic steps such as pirouettes and entrechats. Since the Imperial Theatres would not allow the dancers to perform barefoot as he wished, they were costumed in tights painted with toes. Anna Pavlova, then a rising star of the Imperial Ballet, performed the 'Dance of the Seven Veils'.

Fokine's *Chopiniana* (1907) was originally a series of dramatic or character dances performed to piano pieces by Frédéric Chopin. The germ of Fokine's later version of the ballet was the waltz danced by Pavlova in a long white tutu designed by Léon Bakst (1866–1924; later a leading designer for Diaghilev's Ballets Russes) after a print of Taglioni as the Sylphide. In 1908 the whole female ensemble, identically dressed in white tutus, danced to a different selection of Chopin's pieces, with a single male dancer, Nijinsky, moving dreamily among them. The ballet was renamed *Les Sylphides* in 1909

Overleaf *50* The rebellious Prodigal (Rudolf Nureyev) leaves his father and sisters in the opening scene of George Balanchine's *Prodigal Son (first performed 1929), one of Diaghilev's last successes. Georges Rouault's original set designs, which have a glowing stained-glass quality, are still used.*

as a tribute to Taglioni. A plotless ballet, it creates and sustains a mood of poetic reverie.

In 1907 Fokine made the acquaintance of Alexandre Benois, who had suggested the scenario of a ballet Fokine had choreographed, *Le Pavillon d'Armide*. Benois, a painter with a lively interest in all the arts, in turn introduced him to Serge Diaghilev (1872–1929), who was planning to produce a season of Russian opera and ballet in Paris. Diaghilev had come to the ballet rather belatedly, for he had first made his name as the organizer of several important art exhibitions in Russia and Western Europe, and as the editor of the periodical *Mir Iskusstva* [*The World of Art*], which he had founded in 1898. He briefly worked for the Imperial Theatres as an official in charge of special missions, including the editing of the Annual of the Imperial Theatres, which he made into a thing of unusual beauty. His first exhibition of Russian art in Paris in 1906 was so well received that he followed it with concerts of Russian music in 1907 and Modeste Mussorgsky's opera *Boris Godunov* in 1908. Benois, whose passion for ballet had been inflamed by Virginia Zucchi, persuaded him that Russian ballet also deserved to be seen in the west.

Attracted by Fokine's progressive ideas, Diaghilev engaged him as the chief choreographer of the first season of the Ballets Russes, and assembled for him a company of dancers from the Imperial Theatres of St Petersburg and Moscow. He also engaged a number of Russian singers, including the basso Feodor Chaliapin, who had scored a triumph in *Boris Godunov*, and the chorus of Moscow's Bolshoi Opera. Contrary to Diaghilev's hopes, however, this ambitious enterprise was not granted financial support from the Imperial Theatres, and he had to seek backing from private patrons in France.

The Ballets Russes burst upon Paris in 1909 with the force of a revelation. The enervated ballet of Western Europe could offer nothing comparable. The company was led by the ballerinas Tamara Karsavina (1885–1978), a dancer of great beauty and intelligence, and Pavlova (1881–1931), whose fluent dancing was suffused with dramatic fire. The Parisian audience, which had well-nigh forgotten what good male dancing could be, was enthralled by Nijinsky (c.1889–1950) and Adolph Bolm (1884–1951). Nijinsky's legendary elevation and ability to 'hover' in the air were demonstrated that first season in Fokine's *Pavillon d'Armide* and Petipa's 'Blue Bird' pas de deux from *The Sleeping Beauty*. Fokine's 'Polovtsian Dances' from the third act of Alexander Borodin's opera *Prince Igor* (which Diaghilev presented with both singing and dancing) provided Bolm with his greatest role: as the warrior chief, he projected a virility and fierce energy which was then unknown to Parisian ballet.

51, 52 The Ballets Russes was a source of inspiration to many artists: Rodin's bronze statuette of Nijinsky (1912) captures the dancer's somewhat fey, otherworldly quality. Adolph Bolm, in contrast, was characterized by a ferocious masculine vigour: this photograph shows him in his most famous role, a warrior chief in Fokine's 'Polovtsian Dances' from Prince Igor *(1909).*

The 1909 season also included Fokine's poetic *Les Sylphides*, but although it was well received, the astute Diaghilev immediately grasped that what the public really wanted were ballets like *Cléopâtre*, a revised version of Fokine's earlier *Une Nuit d'Égypte* (1908). Its plot was admittedly slender: a young man (Fokine) is granted a single night of love with the fabled Egyptian queen (Ida Rubinstein), on condition that he drink poison on the morrow; his faithful lover (Pavlova) mourns his death. Bakst's setting, with its monumental columns and statues, blended exoticism and grandeur. Although Rubinstein was not a professional dancer, her striking beauty and unusually tall, slender figure made an indelible impression upon the audience. For her first entrance in *Cléopâtre*, she was carried on in a mummy case and seductively unwrapped from the many-coloured veils that swathed her.

From the first, western writers and artists took an avid interest in the Ballets Russes. An early admirer was the multi-talented Jean Cocteau, who actively contributed to the company by designing posters of Karsavina and Nijinsky in *Le Spectre de la Rose* (1911) and later wrote scenarios for the ballets

53 *With her husband, Mikhail Larionov, Natalia Gontcharova became one of Diaghilev's major designers. Her backdrop for* Le Coq d'Or *(1914) shows the influence of Russian peasant art.*

54 *Yards of gauzy fabric and ever-changing coloured lights transformed Loie Fuller into an insubstantial creature of flame, mist or foam. Photographs give only a dim impression of her magic, which is best conveyed by the artists she captivated, such as Henri de Toulouse-Lautrec, who made this lithograph in 1893.*

Parade (1917), Le Train Bleu (1924) and others. Among the western artists who drew, painted, or sculpted dancers of the Ballets Russes in its early years were John Singer Sargent, Auguste Rodin, Emile-Antoine Bourdelle and Marc Chagall.

Diaghilev revived Cléopâtre's theme of sex and violence for a major offering of the 1910 season, Schéhérazade, which again linked Fokine and Bakst as collaborators. Set to a symphonic poem by Nicolas Rimsky-Korsakov, the ballet depicted an orgy in an oriental harem. Zobeide, the shah's favourite wife (Rubinstein), succumbs to the embraces of the tigerish Golden Slave (Nijinsky). Returning unexpectedly, the shah orders the wholesale massacre of his unfaithful wives and their lovers. The death-throes of the Golden Slave were particularly spectacular: Nijinsky is said to have spun on his head, anticipating the break-dancing fad of the 1980s. Bakst's decor sealed his reputation as a purveyor of barbaric splendour. His unusual colour combinations, especially the pairing of blue and green, were much imitated; in fact, Cléopâtre and Schéhérazade together launched a contemporary mania for exoticism in fashion and interior decoration.

The Firebird (1910) was created by 'committee', a method of collaboration much used during the early or 'Russian' years of the Ballets Russes, when Diaghilev's associates were drawn from a close-knit circle of Russian friends. The scenario was devised by Benois, Fokine, the designer Alexander Golovine and others; Fokine also worked closely with Igor Stravinsky, who had been commissioned to compose the score, his first for ballet. The story, a composite of several Russian folk tales, told how the supernatural Firebird helped Prince Ivan vanquish the evil sorcerer Kastchei and win a beautiful princess for his bride. Karsavina's flashing, fluttering Firebird was dressed not in a tutu but in oriental pantaloons, reflecting the fashion started by Bakst's designs.

Similarly Russian in its theme and creators was Petrouchka (1912). Stravinsky's score was inspired by the Russian puppet Petrouchka, who traditionally appeared at the Butter Week fairs that preceded Lent. Benois's set vividly captured the look of such a fair, and Fokine's choreography made it come alive with a number of typical characters: peddlers, street-dancers, nursemaids, coachmen, a performing bear and so on. The action centres on the sinister Magician (Enrico Cecchetti) and his three puppets: the pathetic Petrouchka (Nijinsky), the Ballerina (Karsavina), and the savage Moor (Alexander Orlov). Petrouchka is a puppet with a soul: he tries to express his love for the Ballerina, but his vehemence frightens her, and she flees to the arms of the Moor. Petrouchka is ultimately 'killed' by the jealous Moor, but his indomitable spirit returns to shriek defiance at the Magician. Nijinsky's Petrouchka, an unattractive object with turned-in limbs and a crudely

55 *Fokine, as Prince Ivan, captures a shimmering magical creature (Karsavina)* in The Firebird *(1910). The designer, Bakst, conceived the Firebird not as a dancer in a tutu but as an exotic Oriental temptress.*

painted face, demonstrated his uncanny ability to transform himself into the characters he portrayed.

Le Spectre de la Rose (1911), an extended pas de deux created by Fokine to Carl Maria von Weber's *Invitation to the Dance*, was inspired by two lines from a poem by Gautier: 'Je suis le spectre d'une rose/Que tu portais hier au bal.' A young girl (Karsavina) returns home from a ball with a rose given her by an admirer. As she dozes in an armchair, the spirit of the rose (Nijinsky) soars in through the window, whirls her about in an intoxicating waltz, then leaps out of the room, seemingly rising into the sky. This final leap, which Nijinsky timed so that his descent was not seen by the audience, completed the illusion of an insubstantial airborne creature, the male equivalent of Taglioni's Sylphide.

In later years ballets such as these came to be looked upon as models for the ideal ballet, representing the complete union of dance, music, drama and design. The period of Fokine's dominance of the Ballets Russes is sometimes viewed as a sort of golden age, never to be equalled by the company's later achievements. Fokine was at the peak of his powers at this time; none of his subsequent works approached the calibre of *Les Sylphides*, *The Firebird* or *Petrouchka*, and none has survived in the international repertory as long as these three ballets.

Despite the success of Fokine's work Diaghilev began to look about for a new choreographer, whom he found in Nijinsky, who was his lover as well as his principal male dancer. In 1910 Nijinsky had begun to choreograph a ballet to Claude Debussy's tone poem *L'Après-midi d'un faune*, working out the movements with his sister Bronislava Nijinska (1891–1972), also a member of the company. Diaghilev decided to present this ballet during the 1912 season.

Nijinsky cast all of its movements in a highly stylized form that many spectators found more evocative of ancient Egypt than Greece, since it utilized a twisted position of the body that presented the torso laterally and the head, legs and feet in profile. Nijinska later explained, however, that her brother wished to evoke archaic Greece rather than the classical Greece preferred by Fokine and Duncan. In a sense Nijinsky's choreography was simply the logical extension of Fokine's dictum that a new movement style should be created for each ballet.

The ballet's plot was simple: a faun lazing on a slope on a golden afternoon catches sight of a group of seven nymphs, the tallest of whom disrobes to bathe in a stream. Though the others flee at his approach, she remains behind long enough to link arms momentarily with him. Then she too runs away, dropping her veil, which the faun retrieves. Spreading it on the ground, he sensuously lowers himself upon it. The first performance of *L'Après-midi d'un*

56 The dancers moved in parallel paths across the stage in Nijinsky's L'Après-Midi d'un faune *(1912) in order to evoke the flat appearance of the ancient Greek bas-reliefs and vase-paintings that had inspired the choreographer (at right).*

faune gained a great deal of notoriety because of the alleged obscenity of the faun's closing movement as he lay down on the veil. Gaston Calmette, the editor of the journal *Le Figaro*, published a scathing attack upon the ballet, which was rebutted by the sculptor Auguste Rodin, who compared Nijinsky's dancing to the beauty of ancient frescoes and sculpture.

An even greater scandal, however, greeted Nijinsky's *The Rite of Spring* [*Le Sacre du Printemps*] in 1913. This time Stravinsky's music as well as Nijinsky's choreography incurred the public's displeasure. The idea for the ballet originated with Stravinsky and Nicolas Roerich, a painter whose fascination with ancient Russia had led to an interest in archaeological research. The scenario they envisioned was uncompromisingly harsh, depicting a primitive world ruled by superstition and fear. The action takes place in prehistoric times among a hypothetical Russian tribe, which celebrates the coming of spring by compelling a chosen maiden to sacrifice herself by dancing until she dies of exhaustion.

Once again Nijinsky abandoned the academic ballet technique and devised a novel type of movement. The illusory lightness and effortlessness of the classical ballet was replaced by a sense of heaviness; symmetry was eliminated; and the primeval quality of the score was expressed through repetitive passages of walking, stamping and heavy jumps. The dancers found Stravinsky's music extremely difficult to count although Diaghilev had engaged Marie Rambert to help analyze the score. She was a student of Emile Jaques-Dalcroze's eurhythmics, a method of musical training through movement that had gained considerable currency in the early part of the century.

The audience reacted violently to the premiere of *The Rite of Spring*. In addition to the shouts, hisses and catcalls that virtually drowned out the orchestra, fights broke out between members of the audience, some of whom considered the ballet a deliberate affront to art. Despite the chaos in the auditorium, Diaghilev, always a canny showman, was pleased by the publicity value of a scandal.

Although many of his contemporaries considered Nijinsky's experiments an artistic dead-end, his innovative ideas have won greater respect today. Unfortunately, his promise as a choreographer was never fulfilled. In 1913, while the company was touring South America without Diaghilev (who had a superstitious fear of crossing water), Nijinsky was married and promptly dismissed from the company by Diaghilev. Nijinsky later rejoined the company for its 1916–17 tours, and staged the ballet *Till Eulenspiegel* in 1916, but it achieved neither the acclaim nor the outrage of his previous choreography. Shortly afterwards he was incapacitated by the insanity that haunted him until his death in 1950. His name, however, continues to be recognized, even by many who have never seen a ballet, as the greatest male dancer the world has known.

The first phase of the Ballets Russes came to an end around 1914, with the departures of Nijinsky and Fokine, who left after many disagreements with Diaghilev. Although Diaghilev never entirely ceased to employ Russian themes or collaborators, after 1914 his artistic policy grew more cosmopolitan in outlook (see chapter 7). He no longer felt that his primary mission was to show Russian art to the west; however, having once made the Ballets Russes a leader of fashion, he was determined to maintain this position. Yet his place in history was already secure. Under his direction, the Ballets Russes had proven to the west that ballet could capture the imagination of the public and command the respect of other artists. The 'Russian years' of the Ballets Russes had indeed reforged the art of ballet.

57 *The artist Valentine Hugo made many action sketches of the Ballets Russes in performance. Here she depicts moments from the dance of the Chosen Maiden in Nijinsky's* The Rite of Spring *(1913).*

CHAPTER SIX

First Steps towards a New Form

Ballet in America in the late 19th century mirrored the state of contemporary European ballet: an increasing emphasis on technical virtuosity and visual spectacle had resulted in the loss of expressional content and depth. Ballet scenes often formed a part of sprawling extravaganzas calculated to dazzle the eye with the splendour and ingenuity of their settings, costumes and stage effects. In this context, dance became little more than an extension of the decorative scheme: entertaining, enjoyable and undemanding.

The Black Crook (1866), the most famous American example of this type of production (it is often called the first musical comedy), was extremely popular with the public: after an initial sixteen-month run, it was repeatedly revived until as late as 1903. Its Faustian story of a man who makes a pact with the devil was recounted through dialogue, songs and elaborately staged dances, including a 'Pas de Naiad [sic]' set in a stalactite-hung grotto. Although it featured some fine dancers, led by the Italian ballerinas Marie Bonfanti and Rita Sangalli, some of its imitators degenerated into mere 'leg shows', known more for the scanty costumes of their dancers than for any pretensions to artistic merit.

Few alternatives were available to aspiring dancers of the period. Vaudeville offered opportunities mainly to male performers of 'speciality' dances, most of which were based on clog dancing (a dance in wooden-soled shoes, similar to tap dancing) or other folk forms. Female dancers performed acrobatics, high kicks or skirt dancing, which had been brought into vogue by the English dancer Kate Vaughan in the 1870s. It derived its name from the long skirt that the dancer manipulated as she executed steps taken from ballet, clog dancing, Spanish dancing and the can-can.

This limited range of choices spurred three Americans, Loie Fuller (1862–1928), Isadora Duncan (1877–1927) and Ruth St Denis (1879–1968), to seek new forms of dancing. Each had had some early experience with existing forms of dancing, but failed to find them artistically fulfilling. Each considered herself an artist rather than a mere entertainer, and each in turn attracted the notice of other artists: writers, musicians, painters and sculptors. Paradoxically, Fuller and Duncan first won widespread acceptance not in the New World but in the Old.

87

58 Isadora Duncan, seen here in her dance the Marseillaise *(1915), embodied the concept of individual freedom both in her life and in her art.*

Fuller devised a type of dance that focused on the shifting play of lights and colours on the voluminous skirts or draperies she wore, which she kept in constant motion principally through movements of her arms, sometimes extended with wands concealed under her costumes. She eschewed the technical virtuosity of ballet, perhaps because her dance training was minimal. Although her early theatrical career had included stints as an actress, she was not primarily interested in storytelling or expressing emotions through dance; the drama of her dancing emanated from its visual effects.

Although she discovered and introduced her art in the U.S., she achieved her greatest glory in Paris, where she was engaged by the Folies Bergère in 1892 and soon became 'La Loïe', the darling of Parisian audiences. Many of her dances represented elements or natural objects – Fire, the Lily, the Butterfly, and so on – and thus accorded well with the fashionable Art Nouveau style, which emphasized nature imagery and fluid, sinuous lines. Her dancing also attracted the Symbolist poets and painters, for it appealed to their liking for mystery, their belief in art for art's sake and their efforts to synthesize form and content.

Fuller had scientific leanings and constantly experimented with electrical lighting (which was then in its infancy), coloured gels, slide projections and other aspects of stage technology. She invented and patented special arrangements of mirrors and concocted chemical dyes for her draperies. Her interest in colour and light paralleled the researches of several artists of the period, notably Georges Seurat, famed for his pointillist paintings. One of her major inventions was underlighting, in which she stood on a pane of frosted glass illuminated from beneath. This was used particularly effectively in her *Fire Dance* (1895), performed to the music of Richard Wagner's 'Ride of the Valkyries'. The dance caught the eye of the artist Henri de Toulouse-Lautrec, who depicted it in a lithograph.

As her technological expertise grew more sophisticated, so did the other aspects of her dances. Although she gave little thought to music in her earliest dances, she later used scores by Gluck, Beethoven, Schubert, Chopin and Wagner, eventually graduating to Stravinsky, Fauré, Debussy and Mussorgsky, composers who were then considered progressive. Her dances began to address more ambitious themes such as *The Sea*, in which her dancers invisibly agitated a huge expanse of silk, played upon by coloured lights. Always open to new inventions, she befriended Marie and Pierre Curie upon their discovery of radium, and created a *Radium Dance* that simulated the phosphorescence of the element. She both appeared in films – then in an early stage of development – and made them herself; the hero of her fairy-tale film *Le Lys de la Vie* (1919) was played by René Clair, later a leading French film director.

At the Paris Exposition Universelle in 1900 she had her own theatre where, in addition to her own dances, she presented pantomimes by the Japanese actress Sada Yacco. She assembled an all-female company at this time, and established a school around 1908, but neither survived her. Although she is remembered today chiefly for her innovations in stage lighting, her activities also touched her compatriots Duncan and St Denis. She sponsored Duncan's first continental appearances. Her theatre at the Paris Expo was visited by St Denis, who found new ideas about stagecraft in Fuller's work and fresh sources for her orientalism in Sada Yacco's plays. In 1924 St Denis paid tribute to Fuller with the duet *Valse à la Loie*.

Isadora Duncan was arguably more than a dancer: she was the symbol of female longings, well-hidden or perhaps even unconscious, for emancipation from the traditional roles of wife and mother, for sexual freedom and personal fulfilment. Her life was of a piece with her dancing in that both placed natural instincts above the dictates of convention. Yet despite the atmosphere of sensationalism that surrounded her during her lifetime and persisted after her death, Duncan was a serious artist with well-defined goals. She sought the wellsprings of dance, which she found in the inner impulse, centred in the solar plexus, that initiates all movement. Nature was her inspiration and her guide. In advocating naturalness, however, she did not intend to abolish formal structure or order for, as she observed, the forms of natural objects reveal design. Rather, she opposed anything that was contrary to nature, among which she classed the turned-out positions of the feet in academic ballet. She found ideas in natural phenomena such as the movement of wind and waves, and her dancing drew upon ordinary actions such as walking, running, skipping and jumping: the normal 'movement repertory' of human beings.

Her dances were characterized by simplicity and economy of means, qualities that applied not only to her choreography but to her themes, scenery and costumes. She had no use for the complicated stories and numerous characters that were prevalent in the ballets of the time, but wanted her dances to speak more directly and intimately to the viewer. Her subject was the soul: universal emotions, responses and aspirations. Much of her dancing predicated her belief in positive human attributes such as the thirst for beauty and harmony, and courage and endurance under travail.

She scorned the elaborately detailed realistic stage settings that had come into fashion during the 19th century; instead she used a backdrop of simple grey-blue or blue curtains. In this her ideas coincided with those of progressive stage designers such as Adolphe Appia and Edward Gordon Craig, who were then evolving a new approach to stagecraft, economical in its means yet all the more telling in its effects. She rejected the ballerina's tutu and pointe shoes, as well as the corset that was then a standard item of feminine attire. The 'little Greek tunic' that she adopted instead was probably inspired by her early fascination with ancient Greece, which was shared and encouraged by her family. Many of her dances were performed without shoes, with the result that her new dance form was labelled 'barefoot dancing' by some of her contemporaries. Her dances used music of the highest quality: Bach, Beethoven, Brahms, Chopin, Schubert, Tchaikovsky and others. She was often criticized for using concert music for the lowly purpose of accompanying the dance, so strong was the belief that dance music was an inferior genre.

Duncan was born in California, where her interest in dance was fostered at an early age by her unconventional, theatre-loving family. In 1896 she was engaged by Augustin Daly's New York-based theatrical company, with which she appeared in bit roles. At this time she also took ballet lessons with Marie Bonfanti, a former star of *The Black Crook*. She left Daly's company in 1898 to strike out on her own and began to perform in the salons of wealthy socialites. Wearing her 'little Greek tunic' she enacted miniature dance-dramas such as *Narcissus* to music by Ethelbert Nevin, and danced to recited quatrains from *The Rubáiyát of Omar Khayyám*.

In 1899 she and her family moved to London, where her style began to mature under the influence of men of culture such as the artist Charles Hallé and J. Fuller-Maitland, the music critic of the London *Times*, who encouraged her to use great works of art and music as sources. Her dance *Primavera*, inspired by Botticelli's painting, dates from this time, as do her early compositions to music by Chopin and Gluck. In the museums of London and Paris she studied ancient Greek art, which confirmed her ideas on the beauty of natural movement. She did not, however, visit Greece itself until 1903, after she had made her name as a dancer.

In 1902 she met Fuller, who sponsored her independent concerts in Vienna and Budapest, thereby launching her continental career. She was immediately acclaimed by German audiences, but with the exception of a few admirers such as Rodin and Bourdelle (who saw in her the embodiment of the ancient world), the Parisians held aloof until 1909, when her performances ran concurrently with the first season of the Ballets Russes. Her first visit to Russia was made in 1904, when she was seen by Fokine, Diaghilev and other leaders of Russia's dance world. Upon returning to the west she started her first school at Grünewald, Germany, providing her young female charges with free upkeep as well as instruction in dancing. In 1908 she returned to the U.S. for the first time since her departure in 1899, and concluded her visit with triumphal performances of Gluck's *Iphigenia in Aulis* at the Metropolitan Opera House in New York City.

59 *Something of Isadora Duncan's fleetness and lightness, qualities noted by many observers, can be seen in this photograph of her, dancing in a Greek theatre in 1904.*

Duncan's daughter and son, both born out of wedlock, were drowned in 1913 as the result of an automobile accident, and her life and art were irrevocably scarred by the tragedy. The joyful lyricism of her early years gave way to more sombre emotions and a heightened awareness of the woes of the world. Two famous dances of this period, the *Marseillaise* (1915) and the *Marche Slave* (1916), vividly portrayed the resilience of the human spirit in the face of adversity. Both have been called dances of social protest because they implicitly refer to historical struggles against tyranny and oppression, the French Revolution and the Russian uprising of 1905. Yet she could also show how strength could be tempered by tenderness, as in Schubert's *Ave Maria* (1914), in which she portrayed the Virgin Mary surrounded by angels.

58

Unquenchably idealistic, Duncan enthusiastically accepted an invitation to establish a school in Soviet Russia in 1921. Although she visited the school only periodically, the students made good progress under the tutelage of Irma, a former Grünewald student and one of her adopted daughters. They presented many performances both in Russia and abroad. In Russia Duncan married the poet Sergei Esenin, whom she brought to visit the west. Her association with him and with Soviet Russia did her no service in the eyes of the conservative American public, which labelled her a Bolshevik. The last years of her life are often depicted as a sordid descent into alcoholism, overweight (no small tragedy to a dancer) and nymphomania. She died in an automobile accident, strangled by her scarf, in 1927.

Her work was carried on by her six eldest pupils, Irma, Anna, Maria-Theresa, Lisa, Erica and Margot, who were nicknamed the Isadorables when they began to perform in public. They started schools in Europe and the U.S. to teach her technique and choreography. Interest in Duncan technique reached its peak during the 1940s but waned thereafter, although a renaissance may be occurring in the more historically-minded 1980s.

Ruth St Denis, the youngest of the trio of American dancers, was destined to have more direct impact on American dance than either of her predecessors. Born Ruth Dennis, she was raised in New Jersey on a heady mixture of feminism, dress reform, Christian Science and theosophy (a western religion incorporating the Hindu ideas of karma and reincarnation). At an early age she learned exercises based upon François Delsarte's system of analyzing body gesture and movement in relation to emotional and spiritual states. These exercises had become the rage in America, where they were published and turned into a theatrical form by Genevieve Stebbins. St Denis saw her perform in 1892, and the strongly dynamic quality of Stebbins's drills laid the groundwork for her own technique.

St Denis began her theatrical career, however, by performing in more traditional genres: acrobatics, high kicking and skirt dancing. She studied ballet and Spanish dancing and appeared as an actress in the theatrical company of David Belasco, who facetiously 'canonized' her, thus providing her with her stage name. According to legend, the image of an enigmatic goddess on a poster for Egyptian Deities Cigarettes changed the course of her artistic life by inspiring her to exploit the Mysterious East – then much in vogue in the west – as source material for her dances. Her first foray into orientalism, however, was not Egyptian but Indian. Drawing upon books, photographs and her memories of an East Indian sideshow at Coney Island, she created the dance *Radha* (1906) to music from Delibes's opera *Lakmé*. In Hindu mythology, Radha is the milkmaid lover of the god Krishna. St Denis turned her into a temple goddess celebrating a ritual of the five senses. Though her choreography made no pretence to authenticity, her supple bendings and ecstatic whirls seemed inexpressibly exotic to audiences of the day, particularly society women, who were fascinated by anything oriental. St Denis's Indian programme also included *The Incense*, famous for the seemingly boneless rippling of her arms, and *The Cobras*, in which each arm represented a writhing, darting serpent.

In May 1906 she crossed the Atlantic in search of new audiences. In Europe, like Fuller and Duncan before her, she won the admiration of artists and intellectuals: the Viennese poet Hugo von Hofmannsthal became a particularly close friend and ally. She studied Indian art and artifacts in museums and created several new dances, among them *The Nautch* (1908), the first of her many evocations of Indian street dancers. The choreography, derived at several removes from India's Kathak style, utilized rhythmic stamping accentuated by ankle bells, whirling, and sinuous arm and head gestures. Later versions of this dance incorporated a spoken patter in 'Indian' and a demand for alms, followed by an elaborate mime of the dancer's contempt upon receiving none from the audience.

St Denis returned to the United States in 1909. She was able to realize, in the following year, her long-cherished dream of creating an Egyptian work. *Egypta* was an ambitious full-length production performed by a cast of fifty dancers and musicians, led by St Denis in the roles of Egypta, the goddess Isis and a palace dancer. Although it did not win favour as a whole, the 'Dance of Day', in which Egypta mimes the diverse activities of peasants, fishermen, priests, warriors and so on, proved to be extremely popular as an independent entity.

St Denis's meeting in 1914 with Ted Shawn (1891–1972), who became her partner and husband, was a crucial event for American dance. Shawn, a former theology student, had begun his professional dancing career as an exhibition ballroom dancer. In St Denis he found a kindred spirit, for they both shared the belief that dance could become a form of religious expression and an integral part of human life. To achieve this goal Shawn, who possessed business acumen as well as ambition, masterminded the establishment of a school dedicated to the loftiest principles of the art of the dance. Founded in Los Angeles in 1915, it was christened Denishawn in the following year, deriving this sobriquet from the winning entry in a contest for the name of a ballroom dance.

60, 61 *Ruth St Denis and Ted Shawn drew their inspiration from many cultures. Radha, first performed by St Denis in 1906 (left), was an exotic if not entirely authentic evocation of Hindu temple dancing. She and Shawn are said to have performed their ancient Egyptian* Dance of Rebirth *(1916) more than 2,500 times (right).*

The Denishawn school offered its students a richly varied curriculum, including ballet (performed without shoes), free-flowing exercises for the arms and torso, ethnic and folk dances, Dalcroze eurhythmics and Delsarte exercises. These classes were supplemented by dance history and philosophy (the latter taught by St Denis, who prided herself on her ability to inspire her students). Denishawn was clearly more than a dance academy intent on transmitting technique: it was a kind of utopia devoted to cultivating harmony between the body, mind and spirit.

In 1916 the entire school took part in *A Dance Pageant of Egypt, Greece, and India* at the open-air Greek Theatre in Berkeley. The production included *Tillers of the Soil*, a duet reminiscent of the 'Dance of Day' from *Egypta*, in which St Denis and Shawn enacted the labours of an Egyptian peasant couple. At the end of the day's work the two quietly walked off stage, the woman resting her head against the man's shoulder. This tribute to the universal human experiences of work and love was performed by St Denis and Shawn for many years. Also on the programme was Shawn's first all-male piece, *Pyrrhic Dance*, anticipating the formation of his Men Dancers group in the 1930s. Making her debut among other Denishawn students was a young dancer named Martha Graham, whose talent had been recognized by Shawn.

The Denishawn company, which drew its dancers from the school, combined showmanship with highminded ideals. St Denis and Shawn were its leading dancers and chief choreographers. Under Shawn's influence, the predominantly oriental subject matter used by St Denis was expanded to include other countries and periods – Amerindian, American, Spanish, North African and so on – thus earning Denishawn a name for eclecticism. Like St Denis's earlier works, these dances made no claim to authenticity; they aimed to capture the spirit rather than the letter of the cultures they depicted. They served, however, to give American audiences a foretaste of ethnic dance styles at a time when such dances were rarely seen on stage. Many of Denishawn's productions also reintroduced the narrative element that had been largely ignored by Fuller and Duncan. Although Denishawn's spectacular sets and costumes rivalled those of the ballet of the period, its purposes were more serious and spiritual in nature: it aimed to uplift as well as entertain.

Notable productions included Shawn's Amerindian solo *Invocation to the Thunderbird* (1917), an athletic rain-making ritual danced in an authentic feathered war bonnet. Charles Weidman, a gifted dancer-mime who had come to the school in 1919, danced the solo *Danse Américaine* (1923) choreographed by Shawn, skilfully creating the illusion of a stage full of people as he rolled dice, played baseball and wooed a pretty girl with a combination of clog, soft-shoe and 'eccentric' dancing. In the climactic scene of Shawn's highly successful Aztec-Toltec dance drama *Xochitl* (1920), the maiden Xochitl (Graham) defended her virtue from a lustful emperor (Shawn) with such fiery realism that he often emerged bruised from the struggle. St Denis's taste for orientalism was carried to its height in the lavishly produced *Ishtar of the Seven Gates* (1923), in which she played a Babylonian goddess who descends into the underworld to reclaim her lover (Shawn).

Yet Denishawn was not entirely devoted to role-playing and fancy dress. St Denis invented what she called 'musical visualizations', which attempted to reflect the structure of the musical composition without recourse to narrative or the interpretation of emotions. She was aided in her experiments by Doris Humphrey, who had come to the school in 1917 with a considerable background of dance training. Although Humphrey had originally intended to be a teacher, St Denis encouraged her to use her gifts as dancer and choreographer, and the two collaborated on several works. The best known of these was *Soaring* (1920), danced to Robert Schumann's *Aufschwung: Fantasiestücke*. A group work for a soloist and four women, this dance utilized a large billowing scarf, which the dancers manipulated under coloured lights to create changing images of waves and clouds in a manner reminiscent of the dances of Fuller.

The company's musical director was Louis Horst, who also served as accompanist, composer, conductor and arranger. His musical taste and willingness to experiment strongly influenced American dance, first through Denishawn and later through Graham (see chapter 8). He improved the quality of the music used by Denishawn, and encouraged both St Denis and Shawn to commission new scores by American composers.

The Denishawn company made numerous tours in the 1910s and 1920s, including a trip to Asia. In a period when performing opportunities were limited, it played the vaudeville circuit, formed part of a touring company of the Ziegfeld Follies, and gave concerts in Lewisohn Stadium. But it contrived to expand the horizons of American audiences both by giving them glimpses of the cultures of other times and places and by showing them a dance form (other than ballet) that took itself seriously as an art.

Financial difficulties and the separation of St Denis and Shawn brought Denishawn to an end in the early 1930s. It had made its mark upon American dance not only through its own productions but by providing training and performing experience to the next generation of American dancers, notably Graham, Humphrey, and Weidman (see chapter 8). St Denis and Shawn both continued their crusade for the dance. St Denis devoted herself to the union of dance and religion; a major project was her Rhythmic Choir, which danced in churches. Shawn's new company, Ted Shawn and His Men Dancers, was dedicated to proving that dancing was a highly masculine activity. The company toured widely in works such as *Labor Symphony* (1934) and *Kinetic Molpai* (1935), a plotless dance of resurrection and celebration. Shawn's choreography for men emphasized strength and athleticism; work movements, warlike drills and the rituals of primitive cultures provided important source material. In 1940 Jacob's Pillow, the Massachusetts farm where Shawn's company was based, played host to a dance festival organized by Mary Washington Ball, a dance teacher. Shawn later became the director of the annual Jacob's Pillow Dance Festival, the first and most enduring of its kind in the U.S. In keeping with Denishawn's ideals, the festival's offerings still include ballet, modern and ethnic dance.

Across the ocean, another dance revolution had begun to brew in Central Europe in the 1910s. It was spearheaded by Rudolf Laban (1879–1958), whose multifaceted explorations into dance and movement gave rise to the dance form called *Ausdrucktanz*, or expressive dance. Many of his innovations were sparked by his interest in physical culture, which was then a craze in Germany. Laban's efforts enlarged the sphere of dance, increasing its importance in recreation, education and therapy. He is best known today for his work as a teacher, theorist and inventor of the system of dance notation that bears his name, Labanotation.

Born in Austria-Hungary, he went to Paris in 1900 to study art. There he became interested in dance and joined a revue troupe that toured in Europe and North Africa. In 1910 he founded a dance school in Ascona, Switzerland, where he developed the prototype of the movement choir, a form of recreational dance that allowed both trained and untrained dancers to move together in harmony. He worked in Zürich during the First World War, delving further into the basic principles of movement, developing his notation system and creating dances for productions by the Dadaists, an anti-art movement that arose in Zürich at this time.

Although Laban's theatrical works are little known today, he was active as a dance director during the 1920s and 30s in Germany and Switzerland. Rejecting the canons of academic ballet, he evolved a form of dance that gave play to a wider range of human movement, for he believed that dance grew out of the life of its time, reflecting ordinary actions such as work movements. The most important component of his new dance form was the flow of movement, which he considered crucial to an understanding of movement in daily life as well. His analysis of movement qualities and their motivations, which he called Eukinetics, enriched his work in the theatre.

Laban established schools in a number of European cities; his most important pupils were the choreographers Mary Wigman (1886–1973) and

62 In works such as Kinetic Molpai *(1935), Ted Shawn and his Men Dancers tried to prove to American audiences that dancing was a pursuit worthy of the red-blooded American male.*

Kurt Jooss (b.1901). He was particularly active in Germany: his Institute of Choreography was based first in Würzburg and later in Berlin, and he staged dances for the first and third German Dancers' Congresses, held in 1927 and 1930. He fled Germany in 1936 after the Nazi Party banned his work, but not before he had seen his concept of the movement choir perverted by the Nazis into a symbol of their desire to manipulate the masses. In 1938 he arrived in England, where he spent the rest of his life. Dartington Hall, where his former students Jooss and Sigurd Leeder had established a school, provided a base for his teaching and research. His later life was devoted to studying the theoretical, educational and practical aspects of movement.

97

Mary Wigman, who first studied with Laban at Ascona in 1910, later recalled him as an inspirational teacher who set his pupils free to follow their own paths. Wigman had gone to Laban via the Dalcroze schools in Dresden and Hellerau, where she had studied the system of musical and movement training called eurhythmics. Laban encouraged her essays into theatrical dance, and she gave the first public performances of her choreography under his auspices in 1914. This debut included the first sketch of her grotesque *Witch Dance*, much of which was danced in a seated position: a far cry from Taglioni's airborne Sylphide. Wigman wore a mask that she has described as a demonic translation of her own features. The sense of evil and animality that emanated from the grasping, clawlike gestures and the earthbound heaviness of the dancer's body were very remote indeed from the contemporary ballet's insubstantial prettiness, Duncan's emphasis upon harmony, or St Denis's glamour. In her book *The Language of Dance* (1963), Wigman confesses that she was initially frightened by the suppressed emotions she unleashed in choreographing this dance.

63, 64 Two German pioneers of modern dance: Rudolf Laban (left), best known as a theorist and educator, began his career as an active and innovative performer and choreographer. His pupil Mary Wigman (right) spurned the decorative prettiness of contemporary ballet in favour of a style that emphasized emotional intensity and strong, stark movements.

65 *Rudolf Laban developed the movement choir as a means of giving both trained and untrained dancers the experience of moving together in harmony. His disciple Albrecht Knust (right) leads the group.*

In many of her later dances Wigman confronted subjects that many people find hard to face whether in the theatre or in real life: the dark side of human nature, the ravages of war, the inevitable coming of old age, the irrevocability of death. The solo 'Face of Night' from her dance cycle *Swinging Landscape* (1929) was a tribute to the German soldiers killed in the First World War, whom she memorialized more explicitly in *Totenmal* (1930), in which a women's chorus mourns their dead, who briefly return to life before being swallowed by death and oblivion. *Song of Fate* (1935), a masked dance, depicted a woman in youth, maturity and old age.

Because of her treatment of such subjects, Wigman is often associated with the German Expressionist painters, who used exaggeration and distortion to convey strong and often unpleasant emotions. (She was a friend of the painter Emil Nolde.) These dances, however, are only one aspect of her repertory. She was also capable of lyricism, as in the 'Pastorale' (from the *Swinging Landscape* cycle), which opened with her lying on the ground, as though reclining in a sunlit field. She also explored the formal aspects of dance: in *Ceremonial Figure* (1925) her bell-shaped costume, invented by sewing a child's hoop into the hem of her skirt, compelled her to move within severely limited bounds, which she further constricted by wearing a depersonalizing mask that scarcely allowed her to see. In *Space Shape* (1928), she used a long strip of red silk and grey velvet, fastened at one end to her skirt and the other to a lead-weighted stick, to carve out shapes in space.

Wigman also experimented with musical accompaniments for dance, an interest that had begun in her Dalcroze days and continued during her studies with Laban. She often used percussion instruments such as gongs and drums, in addition to the flute and the piano. Sometimes she danced to a spoken text. She made a distinction between pre-existing music and music created expressly to support the dance; occasionally she discarded music completely and danced in silence. Yet she also choreographed Gluck's *Orpheus and Eurydice* (1947, 1961), Carl Orff's *Carmina Burana* (1943, 1955), and Stravinsky's *The Rite of Spring* (1957).

Wigman's school in Dresden, founded in 1920, turned out many important German modern dancers, among them Hanya Holm, Yvonne Georgi, Gret Palucca, Max Terpis, Margarethe Wallmann and Harald Kreutzberg. She and her company were enthusiastically received during their three tours in the U.S. between 1930 and 1933, and Holm was sent in 1931 to open a Wigman School in New York, thus bringing German modern dance to America. Wigman's activities in Germany were curtailed by the Nazis, who placed her on their blacklist and took over her school. In 1945 she reopened her school first in Leipzig, then in West Berlin, and resumed choreographing.

Another student of Laban, Kurt Jooss, began to study with the master in Stuttgart in 1920 and helped him develop his system of dance notation. He worked as a balletmaster in various German cities, notably in Essen, where in 1928 he founded a company that became the nucleus for the later Ballets Jooss. His choreography blended academic ballet technique (omitting the use of pointes and virtuosic steps such as pirouettes) with the freer, more expressive movements of *Ausdrucktanz*.

The Green Table, which he choreographed in 1932, is a searing indictment of war. Inspired by the medieval image of the Dance of Death, it is dominated by the personification of Death (a role created by Jooss himself), who draws into his grisly procession various victims of war: the soldier, the resistance fighter, the old woman, the young girl sold to a brothel, and even the jackal-like profiteer. The ballet opens and closes with a scene of diplomats in conference around a green baize table: their grotesquely comical masked faces and pompous, self-important gestures (accompanied by light, pattering music in the rhythm of a tango) contrast with the depredations of Death.

Explicit political criticism of this sort could not be welcome in a society dominated by the Nazis. Jooss and his company were forced to leave Germany for England in 1933. The Ballets Jooss toured internationally, presenting a repertory that ranged from the lighthearted *Ball in Old Vienna* (1932) to *The Big City* (1932), the tale of a young girl's disillusionment, but *The Green Table* remained its most popular offering.

66 In the year of its premiere, Kurt Jooss's The Green Table *(1932) won first prize in a choreographic competition held by the Archives Internationales de la Danse in Paris. Still performed today, it has lost none of its impact as a protest against the futility of war.*

Ballet's long dominance of art dance was over. No longer did the public believe that a dancer had to rise to the tips of her toes before her art could be considered either beautiful or highbrow. Duncan, St Denis, Shawn, Wigman and the rest had proven that alternatives were possible. The years of experimentation had not yet ended, and many changes were still in store, but the work of these pioneers had prepared the way for new directions in the art of the dance.

67 Edmund Dulac, who also illustrated fairy tales, drew this impish commentary on the Ballets Russes's production of The Sleeping Princess *(1921): the Good Fairy Bakst leads Prince Charming Diaghilev to the shrine of the Sleeping Princess.*

CHAPTER SEVEN

'Astonish Me'

Ballet did not remain at a standstill during the years when new forms of dance were coming to birth. The spirit of experimentation that had sparked Fokine's reforms reached a peak in the 1920s, affecting many choreographers who worked within the framework of traditional ballet. Some tried to enrich ballet's vocabulary with movements from other sources: social dances, acrobatics, gymnastics and ethnic dances. Others began to renovate the subject matter of dance, introducing themes based on contemporary life. Still others evolved a type of choreography less dependent on narrative and more closely approaching pure dance.

The most conspicuous innovation of the 1920s, however, occurred in the area of stage design. Ballet began to ally itself with progressive movements in the visual arts. The 'Russian years' of the Ballets Russes had prepared the way by breaking with the tradition of using hack composers and designers. The use of modern technology, inspired in part by Loie Fuller's example, enhanced ballet's brave new look: lighting gained in versatility and importance, and new inventions such as film added further dimensions to the ballet stage.

The fascination with stage design occasionally led choreographers to neglect or de-emphasize the human element of their ballets. Dancers were encumbered by figure-concealing costumes; masks hid their facial expressions; and they were sometimes required to imitate machines, which were admired for their speed, precision and energy. This was a radical shift from the classicism of Petipa, which had never denied the essential humanity of the dancers even while demanding from them a physical perfection that bordered on the godlike. Petipa's precepts were not entirely forgotten, however; the style known as the neoclassical ballet built upon and extended his formalism, giving it new interest without violating the rules of clarity and order.

In Russia a period of experimentalism followed the 1917 Revolution. Petipa's ballets had fallen into disfavour because of their association with the imperial court. Their characteristic fairy-tale themes, keyed to an audience nostalgic for the past, seemed out of touch with modern life and values. Post-revolutionary choreographers hoped to remedy this. In order to make ballet available as well as appealing to the masses, they found alternative stages for their works: cabarets, music-halls, circuses, outdoor theatres and the like. Several formed small-scale 'chamber ballet' groups that allowed more creative freedom than the large established companies.

In the vanguard of the Russian experimentalists were Kasian Goleizovsky (1892–1970) and Fyodor Lopukhov (1886–1973). Until recently little has been known in the west about their work. Both were products of the Imperial Ballet School. Goleizovsky's most daring experiments were mounted in the 1920s, many of them with the chamber ballet company that he founded in Moscow. Lopukhov, who was appointed artistic director of the Leningrad State Theatre of Opera and Ballet in 1922, did most of his work for that company.

Goleizovsky, like Laban, believed that the flow of movement was the essential ingredient of dance. In order to re-invigorate the academic technique, he introduced into his choreography elements from gymnastics, acrobatics and popular social dances such as the foxtrot and tango. The intertwining lifts and poses he devised, in combination with the revealing costumes of his dancers, gave his works a strong erotic flavour that he apparently saw no reason to shun: in his programme of 'eccentric dances' in 1923, he imported the scandalous apache dance from Paris.

His interest in jazz led him to use a jazz band to accompany his dances for Vsevolod Meyerhold's multi-media production *D.E.* (1924). The sets for several of his ballets were designed by members of the artistic movement known as Soviet Constructivism, which abandoned illusionism and advocated the use of modern materials and industrial processes. Boris Erdman's set for *Joseph the Beautiful* (1924), for instance, consisted of platforms, scaffolding and stairs that enabled the choreographer to exploit different levels of the stage. The biblical story of Joseph and his brothers was told through a series of poses, and the dancers' bodies were painted in different colours to denote the races they represented (Jews, Egyptians, Ethiopians).

Lopukhov's experiments were less radical, perhaps because of the demands of his position. He was primarily interested in re-examining the relationship between music and the dance, and believed that choreographers should study the orchestral scores of their ballets so that their choreography would reflect musical qualities such as instrumental colour and dynamics. He wanted to replace the dramatic motivation of ballet with a more purely musical impetus: dance should spring from and correspond to the music. His ideas were published in his book *Paths of a Balletmaster* (1925).

Despite the fact that it was given only one performance, his ballet *Tanzsynfonia* [*Dance Symphony*], subtitled *Magnificence of the Universe* (1923), has become the best known of his works, perhaps because it was a forerunner of the plotless ballets that became an important genre in the twentieth century. Danced to Beethoven's Fourth Symphony, *Tanzsynfonia* did not relay a story, though it had an elaborate programme symbolizing the birth of light in the universe, the awakening of nature, the joy of existence and other large-scale concepts. Lopukhov's choreography combined academic ballet technique with acrobatic movements such as the high lifts that later became identified with the Soviet ballet. The youthful cast included the future choreographers George Balanchine and Leonid Lavrovsky.

Both Goleizovsky and Lopukhov created early examples of Soviet political ballets. Two of their ballets had almost identical titles, emanating from the idea of the whirlwind as a cleansing agent. Lopukhov's *Red Whirlwind* (1924) eulogized the achievements of the 1917 Revolution. In the more abstract first 'process' or act, a group of dancers that moved strongly and aggressively were opposed to a more tentative, evasive group. In the second 'process', dissolute elements of society such as robbers and drunks were defeated by the workers. Goleizovsky's *The Whirlwind* (1927) showed the workers triumphing over a king and his decadent fox-trotting subjects.

In Western Europe Diaghilev had embarked upon a period of avant-garde experiment in the late 1910s. With increasing frequency he began to choose his collaborators from among Western European artistic circles, particularly the painters of the modernist School of Paris and the composers known as Les Six. Part of this was due to simple expedience – he had been cut off from his Russian collaborators by the First World War and later by the Revolution – and part to the desire to attract audiences, but he was also motivated by a spirit of real adventurousness, expressed in his famous injunction to Cocteau, 'Astonish me.'

This new era entailed a loss of stability, since a purveyor of novelties must constantly renew his stock. Unlike Bakst and Benois, most of Diaghilev's new designers and composers worked on only one or two ballets. Among the exceptions were the painters Mikhail Larionov (1881–1969) and Natalia Gontcharova (1881–1962). Husband and wife, they had led Russia's avant-garde before leaving the country prior to World War I. Gontcharova's brightly coloured peasant designs, transformed by Cubist principles, enlivened Fokine's ballet *Le Coq d'Or* (1914) and the 1926 revival of *The Firebird*, among others. Larionov's abilities were so highly rated by Diaghilev that he set him to co-choreograph the ballet *Chout* (1921): his sketches of poses and groupings were translated into dance by the dancer Taddeus Slavinsky.

Another frequent collaborator was Pablo Picasso, who first worked with the company in 1917. His Cubist sets and costumes appeared in the ballets *Parade* (1917), *Le Tricorne* (1919), *Pulcinella* (1920) and *Cuadro Flamenco* (1921), and his drop-curtain of two giantesses running on a beach was used

53

for the ballet *Le Train Bleu* (1924). Cubism was probably the most tenacious of the many 'isms' that materialized on the Ballets Russes stage, but others were also represented in the repertory. The Futurist painter Giacomo Balla designed the set and lighting for *Fireworks* (1917), which was not a ballet at all, but a light show accompanied by Stravinsky's composition of the same name. *Romeo and Juliet* (1926), designed by the Surrealists Max Ernst and Joan Miró and choreographed by Nijinska, concluded with an elopement in an airplane. Another Surrealist, Giorgio de Chirico, furnished Balanchine's *Le Bal* (1929) with the columns and statues that often appear in his paintings.

Stravinsky, a veteran of the 'Russian years', continued to compose for the company; other frequent musical contributors included his compatriot Sergei Prokofiev and the French composer Georges Auric, a member of Les Six.

There was, in a sense, a symbiotic relationship between the avant-garde and the Ballets Russes, for the modernists lent the ballet the air of contemporaneity and novelty that Diaghilev prized, while the ballet reciprocated by giving modern art and music wide exposure and publicity. In some cases a genuine cross-fertilization resulted: Balanchine has stated that Stravinsky's neoclassic score for *Apollon Musagète* (1928) taught him valuable lessons about the craft of choreography, such as the idea of family-relationships between movements, and the elimination of superfluities.

The Ballets Russes did not, of course, leap into the modern world overnight; the process was more gradual. Following the departures of Fokine and Nijinsky, Diaghilev began to groom the youthful Léonide Massine (1895–1979), who had joined the company in 1914, as a choreographer. His first ballet, *Le Soleil de Nuit* [*The Midnight Sun*] (1915) utilized elements of Russian folklore similar to those Fokine had used in *The Firebird* and *Petrouchka*. The new spirit of the Ballets Russes was first demonstrated in Massine's *Parade* (1917), which took its name from the sideshow performed outside fairground theatres to lure spectators inside. The score, commissioned from Erik Satie, incorporated real noises such as a ship's siren, an aeroplane engine and pistol shots. Picasso, who designed the sets, proposed the characters called the New York and Parisian Managers, played by dancers wearing enormous Cubist sculptures. Two dancers in a horse costume played the third Manager. The show's other attractions included a pair of acrobats; a Little American Girl who works at a typewriter, jumps onto a moving train, and sinks with the *Titanic*; and a Chinese conjurer (Massine) who breathes fire and swallows an egg in imitation of the conjurers of the music-halls.

One of Massine's most popular ballets was *La Boutique Fantasque* (1919), a fairy tale of dolls that come to life. He and the ebullient Lydia Lopokova (1891–1981) played a pair of cancan-dancing dolls, sweethearts who rebel

68–70 Massine's Parade *(1917), conceived by Cocteau and composed by Satie, was designed by Picasso, whose drop-curtain (top) bore little relation to events on the stage, although its acrobats, musicians and clowns foreshadowed the ballet's fairground setting. The elaborate costumes included a horse (above, left) and a Cubist structure for the Parisian manager (above, right).*

when threatened with separation. He also choreographed delightfully detailed roles for other national types, including two American parents who prudishly shield their children's eyes from the risqué antics of a pair of dancing poodles.

During the company's wartime tours in Spain, Massine studied Spanish dancing and customs. The fruit of his research, *Le Tricorne* [*The Three-Cornered Hat*] (1919), displayed his great genius for character dancing. All his collaborators were Spanish: Manuel de Falla's score, the seed of the ballet, was inspired by Pedro Antonio Alarcón's novel *El Sombrero de tres picos* (1874) and Picasso designed the sets and costumes. The ballet tells the story of a lecherous old corregidor (governor) whose attempt to seduce the miller's beautiful wife (Karsavina) is foiled by her and the miller (Massine). A number of Spanish dances were included, notably the miller's fiery *farucca*; the miller also fought a mock bullfight with the hapless corregidor as his bull. The ballet became one of the most enduring of Massine's works.

When Massine left the Ballets Russes in 1921, the company was once again bereft of a choreographer. Perhaps as a stopgap measure, Diaghilev decided to revive Petipa's *The Sleeping Beauty*, which he retitled *The Sleeping Princess*. Diaghilev's espousal of the classical ballet was rooted to some extent in nostalgia. He engaged Nicholas Sergeyev, formerly a balletmaster in St Petersburg, to reconstruct the choreography. Carlotta Brianza, the first Aurora, played the wicked fairy Carabosse, a role later taken over by the original Carabosse, Enrico Cecchetti. Diaghilev's old friend Bakst designed the scenery and costumes, and Nijinska, who had been working in Soviet Russia, returned to the company to contribute additional choreography to the ballet.

Despite its lavish sets and costumes, and the appearances of a new Russian star, Olga Spessivtseva (b.1895), as Aurora, *The Sleeping Princess* was accounted a failure. Many Ballets Russes fans, having grown fond of modernist fare, found it old-fashioned, almost reactionary. Its five scenes seemed interminably long to audiences accustomed to the one-act ballets popularized by the Ballets Russes itself. London's critics, unable to appreciate the glories of classical dancing, wondered if the company had finally succumbed to artistic exhaustion. Diaghilev's dreams of lucrative returns were shattered as the ballet's run ended in financial loss.

The Sleeping Princess was not a total disaster, however. Diaghilev salvaged from the wreck a popular one-act ballet called *Aurora's Wedding*. More importantly, he found a new choreographer in Nijinska, whose ballet *Les Noces* (1923) must have revived memories of her brother's experiments in *The Rite of Spring*. Danced to Stravinsky's score for four pianos, timpani, percussion and singers, *Les Noces* represents a Russian peasant wedding, yet completely abandons the colour and gaiety usually associated with folkloristic themes. The austere set and simple brown and white costumes designed by Gontcharova portray a world governed by necessity, where marriage is seen as a means of continuing the life of the community. The bride, bridegroom, and their parents are delineated not so much as individuals as celebrants of a universal rite.

Nijinska heightened this abstract quality by placing the women on pointe to give them the elongated silhouette of figures on icons, and emphasizing the symmetry of the groupings. The characters' gestures are formalized and their interaction with one another is, for the most part, rigidly controlled. Yet the strong emotional impact of *Les Noces* is undeniable. The sheer force of many of the movements, such as the jabbing of the women's pointes into the floor and the repeated heavy jumps, conjures up a world of unremitting, back-breaking toil, where strength and endurance are vital for survival.

Nijinska followed the essentially timeless *Les Noces* with two ballets of contemporary life. *Les Biches* (1924), which derives its title from the French word for does (colloquially, young women), depicts the highly ambiguous goings-on at a fashionable house-party. Its shady characters include two young ladies who are more interested in each other than in the musclebound

71, 72 Bakst assiduously researched 18th-century sources for his Sleeping Princess *designs, such as this sketch for Princess Aurora's wedding dress (*left*). In complete contrast was* Les Noces, *in which Gontcharova's austere costumes reflected Nijinska's attempt to convey the raw strength and hardiness of peasant life (*right*).*

athletes who show off for them, and an enigmatic girl (or is she a page boy?) in a short blue velvet tunic and white gloves, who dances a duet with one of the athletes. Armed with pearl necklace and cigarette holder, Nijinska herself played the hostess, a women desperately seeking to recover her lost youth. In spite of its hints of social satire, *Les Biches*, with its score by Francis Poulenc and designs by Marie Laurencin, was well liked by the fashionable audience.

Despite its title *Le Train Bleu* (1924), which Nijinska set to music by Darius Milhaud, does not depict a train but rather its destination, the fashionable resort of Deauville. Dressed in chic sportswear by Chanel, the dancers engage in various sports (swimming, tennis, golf) on a Cubist beach designed by the sculptor Henri Laurens. The ballet highlighted the acrobatic feats of a talented newcomer, the British dancer Anton Dolin (born Patrick Healey-Kay, 1904–83). Nijinska modelled her own role of the tennis player after a real-life champion, Suzanne Lenglen.

In 1925 Nijinska in turn left the company, but this time Diaghilev had two strings to his bow, for in addition to Massine as guest choreographer he had Balanchine (1904–83), who had left Soviet Russia in the preceding year. Between them the two dominated the final years of the Ballets Russes. Balanchine, a graduate of the Petrograd (formerly Imperial) Ballet School, had been infected by the iconoclasm of Lopukhov and Goleizovsky, whose influence showed itself most obviously in his penchant for unconventional movements. While still in Russia he had organized a company called the Young Ballet, three members of which (Alexandra Danilova, Tamara Geva and Nicholas Efimov) had accompanied him to the west.

The first of Balanchine's ballets to be shown in Paris was a revival of Stravinsky's *Le Chant du Rossignol* [*The Song of the Nightingale*] (1925), based on Hans Christian Andersen's fairy tale. The role of the nightingale was danced by Alicia Markova (b.1910), a teenaged British dancer whose name had been Russianized from the more prosaic Marks. In 1927 Balanchine presented *La Chatte*, a modernistic adaptation of a fable by Aesop, danced to a score by the French composer Henri Sauguet. Although the Constructivist scenery and costumes were credited to the brothers Naum Gabo and Anton Pevsner, Pevsner actually designed only the statue of the goddess Aphrodite, who answers a youth's prayers to turn his cat into a woman. *La Chatte*'s principal male role was danced by a rising young Russian dancer, Serge Lifar (1905–86), who was then relatively unformed. Balanchine's choreography not only concealed his technical deficiencies but created many images of startling beauty, such as Lifar's entrance in a 'chariot' formed by his male companions.

Massine's major offering of the 1927 season was *Le Pas d'Acier* [*The Steel Dance*], a depiction of life in Soviet Russia. Its high point was its evocation of

73 A Cubist backdrop by Henri Laurens and modish beachwear by Coco Chanel appealed to the fashionable viewers of Nijinska's Le Train Bleu *(1924), an evocation of chic society in Deauville.*

the throbbing dynamism of a factory. The dancers' repetitive machine-like movements (swinging arms, pounding feet) worked in masterly conjunction with Prokofiev's pulsing score and the whirling wheels and flashing lights of Georgi Yakulov's Constructivist set. Light of various sorts played an important part in Massine's *Ode* (1928), which was based upon an 18th-century poem by Mikhail Lomonosov that likened the Empress Elizabeth to the aurora borealis. The designer, Pavel Tchelitchev, may have been inspired by Loie Fuller's *The Sea*, which he had seen in 1925. Using slide projections, mirrors and a time-lapse film of blossoming flowers, he and Massine devised a spectacle of light and movement. Masked dancers in white all-over tights created a series of geometric shapes with cords; a man danced a duet with a moving ray of light. In another duet, gauze panels diffused the dancers' forms, lending them an insubstantial quality.

Balanchine's *Apollon Musagète*, choreographed in 1928 to Stravinsky's score, depicted the birth of the Greek god Apollo (Lifar) and his encounter with three muses: Calliope, representing poetry; Polyhymnia, mime; and Terpsichore, dance. Each performs a solo symbolizing her special art. The only one to win his approval is Terpsichore (Alice Nikitina), who is rewarded   74

by the privilege of dancing a pas de deux with him. The ballet puzzled an audience accustomed to picturing the god in terms of ancient sculpture. It was Balanchine's first essay into the neoclassic style: despite its firm foundation in the classical ballet, it spices the academic technique with movements such as Apollo's vigorous arm-swings as he 'plays' his lute, his flat-footed shuffling with the muses, and the 'swimming lesson', in which Terpsichore reclines on his back, gracefully moving her arms. Yet these movements are not intended to shock the viewer by violating academic rules but rather to extend the traditional vocabulary of ballet.

50   The last great ballet of the Diaghilev era was Balanchine's *Le Fils prodigue* [*The Prodigal Son*], created to Prokofiev's score in 1929, the year of Diaghilev's death. Adapted from the biblical story, it opens with the prodigal's rebellious departure from home and his seduction by the beautiful but treacherous siren, whose followers rob him. Wretched and remorseful, he drags himself back to his forgiving father. Lifar, in the title role, won a great personal triumph for his miming of the homecoming scene. The prodigal's acrobatic couplings with the tall, coolly erotic siren (Felia Doubrovska) also made a strong impression upon the audience.

These two ballets, now known as *Apollo* and *Prodigal Son*, are Balanchine's only ballets for Diaghilev that have survived to the present day. Though *Apollo* has undergone many changes of costume and scenery, finally arriving at a pared-down simplicity, its choreography has essentially remained the same. *Prodigal Son*, on the other hand, has retained its sets and costumes by Georges Rouault, which are identified with the ballet.

In 1920 the Ballets Russes was confronted by a rival, the Ballets Suédois, organized by a wealthy Swede, Rolf de Maré (1898–1964), with dancers from the Royal Swedish and Royal Danish ballet companies. This company did not attain the longevity of the Ballets Russes, for it lasted only until 1925. Although its sole choreographer, Jean Börlin (1893–1930), also a Swede, created more than twenty ballets, it is better known today for its collaborators than for its choreography. Its librettists, designers and composers included some of the top creative talents in Paris: the poets Blaise Cendrars, Paul Claudel, Cocteau and Riciotti Canudo; the composers Auric, Arthur Honegger, Milhaud, Cole Porter, Poulenc and Satie; and the artists de Chirico, Fernand Léger and Francis Picabia.

Not surprisingly, much of the repertory of the Ballets Suédois was avant-garde in nature, although ballets such as *Dansgille* (1921), based on Swedish folk dances, were extremely popular. Visual design was a strong element in the company's productions, sometimes overpowering the dancing. One of the most striking designs was created by Andrée Parr for *L'Homme et son désir* (1921). The four-tiered stage was occupied by symbolic figures such as the

74 *Balanchine described* Apollon Musagète *(1928) as a turning point in his life because Stravinsky's neoclassic score taught him to reduce his choreography to the most telling essentials. In keeping with this idea, he later abandoned the fanciful set and costumes of the first production, shown here, in favour of a bare stage and simple tunics and tights.*

black-robed Hours of the Night, the Moon and her reflection. Dancers representing musical instruments (cymbals, bells and panpipes) wore fanciful headdresses and masks that concealed their faces and gave them the look of abstractions.

Conceived by Cocteau as a satirical celebration of the bourgeois and the banal, *Les Mariés de la Tour Eiffel* (1921) depicted a wedding party set on a 75 terrace of the Eiffel Tower on Bastille Day. A photographer tries to take pictures, but out of his camera emerge an ostrich, a bathing beauty and a lion; meanwhile, gramophones at either side of the stage comment ironically on the action in the fashion of a Greek chorus. The dancers were encased in elaborate costumes and masks that made it hard for them to hear the music, which united the efforts of five members of Les Six: Auric, Honegger, Milhaud, Poulenc and Germaine Tailleferre.

Börlin's interest in primitive cultures, which was shared by many artists of the early 20th century, inspired *La Création du Monde* (1923). Its source, an African creation myth, was reflected in Milhaud's jazz score and Léger's designs, but most of the choreography was couched in the academic ballet technique. Börlin added a few original touches, however, such as the heron-dancers who moved on stilts.

The company's last production was the Dadaist ballet *Relâche* (1924), whose title means a cancelled performance. There was no recognizable classical dancing in this ballet, the cast of which included a fireman, an elegant lady and nine men who at one point doffed their evening clothes to reveal their long underwear. The backdrop, designed by Picabia (who also wrote the scenario), consisted of row upon row of automobile headlamps, which were brightened and dimmed during the performance. René Clair's film *Entr'acte*, the first to be used in a ballet, was played during the intermission. Following a series of random images, among them the artists Man Ray and Marcel Duchamp playing chess, it culminated with the mock funeral of Börlin, which turns into a comic chase when the hearse runs away.

The Ballets Suédois's intense concentration on design was carried even further by Oskar Schlemmer (1888–1943). Trained as a painter, he began his

75 *An ostrich (centre) pops out of a camera to join the bizarre guests at the wedding party in Cocteau's* Les Mariés de la Tour Eiffel *(1921).*

76 Much of the fascination of Oskar Schlemmer's Triadic Ballet *(1922) lay in its unconventional costumes, which occasionally seemed to deny the humanity of the dancers. At far left is 'The Abstract', a threatening figure of fantasy.*

first experiments in dance in 1910, and composed the preliminary sketches for his *Triadic Ballet* [*Triadisches Ballett*] as early as 1916. In 1921 he joined the faculty of the recently founded Bauhaus school in Weimar, which aspired to create a new union of architecture, crafts and the fine arts. He continued his choreographic work under the auspices of the Bauhaus, producing the *Triadic Ballet* in 1922, followed by his *Bauhaus Dances* in 1926. Between 1925 and 1929 he directed the Theatre Workshop of the Bauhaus in Dessau, the source of many experimental works. In his choreography as well as his art Schlemmer aimed at representing universal, idealized forms. The dancers in the *Triadic Ballet* emerge as depersonalized, occasionally dehumanized figures. Their faces are heavily coated with white make-up or hidden by masks; their arms, legs, and torsos are often padded or completely disguised; even their hands are compressed by thumbless mittens. Though the woman dances on pointe, this too becomes a means of stylization rather than emotional expression. The dancers often resemble articulated dolls or puppets, a quality heightened by the simple, often repetitive movements and lack of emotional interaction. Much of the *Triadic Ballet*'s emotional resonance is supplied by Paul Hindemith's weirdly evocative score. The *Triadic Ballet*'s chief claim to interest lies in the costumes designed by Schlemmer. Many of the female dancer's costumes are variations on the tutu, which is enamelled like a spinning top, vertically raised to frame her upper body, or made of coils of silver wire. Other costumes were inspired by toys or folk art. A few have the inhuman quality of science-fiction creatures: the figure called 'The Abstract', for instance, has a bisected, asymmetrical head; one arm ends in a spike, the other in a golden club.

In a countermovement to the prevailing emphasis on stage design, Anna Pavlova's dancing highlighted her expressiveness, personal magnetism and technical mastery. She had a legendary power to transcend the mediocre choreography and banal themes of much of her repertory. Wherever she performed, her dancing commanded the audience's attention.

Pavlova began her career as one of the Imperial Ballet's most promising young ballerinas. She first appeared outside Russia in 1908, and danced with the Ballets Russes between 1909 and 1911. In 1910 she resigned from the Imperial Ballet and eventually settled in London, where she formed a company largely comprised of English girls with Russianized names. She spent the rest of her life touring Europe, the Americas, Asia, Australia, Egypt and South Africa. In 1915 she appeared in a film, *The Dumb Girl of Portici*, in which she played a mute girl betrayed by an aristocrat.

The most famous dances in her repertory were solos (several choreographed by herself) inspired by natural images: *Dragonfly* (1915), *California Poppy* (1915) and the best known of all, *The Dying Swan*, which Fokine had choreographed for her in 1907. It remained closely identified with her all her life, and she asked for her swan costume a few moments before she died. The choreography was deceptively simple, but Pavlova infused it with unutterable poignancy, her arm movements evoking the beating of wings in a last convulsive effort to fly.

She also performed many 'ethnic' dances, some of which she learned from local teachers during her travels. In addition to the dances of her native Russia, she performed Mexican, Japanese and East Indian dances. Supported by her interest, Uday Shankar, her partner in *Krishna and Radha* (1923), went on to revive the long-neglected art of the dance in his native India.

Pavlova also presented excerpts or abridged versions of ballets from the Imperial Russian repertory. In 1916 she produced a fifty-minute adaptation of *The Sleeping Beauty* in New York City. One of her favourite ballets was *Giselle*, which she considered her direct link to the past, for she had been coached in the role by Petipa, who had assisted Perrot in restaging the ballet in Russia in 1850. The almost frightening intensity of her first-act mad scene contrasted strikingly with the poetry she brought to the second act, when

Giselle appears as a spirit. Pavlova's most important legacy lies in the love for ballet she awakened and the inspiration she gave to many aspiring young dancers and choreographers. Like Taglioni and Elssler before her she made ballet an internationally popular art, extending it far beyond the countries they had visited.

Like all periods of experimentalism, the 1920s engendered a few enduring masterworks and a rather larger number of earnest endeavours that for one reason or another have failed to survive. Despite the short lives of most of their works, the choreographers of the 1920s accomplished some real changes in the ways ballet is produced and perceived. No longer was it an anomaly for serious writers, composers or artists to contribute their talents to the ballet, nor was ballet the only gainer by the transaction. Audiences had become more accustomed to the introduction of novelties in ballet, and could even feel disappointed when offered traditional fare. By stretching the boundaries of the permissible, the 1920s gave ballet valuable room in which to grow and develop.

77 *The poetry of Anna Pavlova's dancing, evinced here in her famous solo* The Dying Swan, *awakened a love of ballet wherever she performed.*

CHAPTER EIGHT

Truly Modern

By the 1920s Denishawn had become an establishment, and in the way of establishments, whether in government or in art, it began to be troubled by dissension in its ranks. With a sense of classical symmetry, the two leading rebels were Martha Graham (b.1894), a protégée of Shawn's, and Doris Humphrey (1895–1958), a protégée of St Denis's. Charles Weidman (1901–75), who worked closely with Humphrey, also joined the rebellion. Their secession had historic consequences, for their post-Denishawn careers gave rise to the theatrical dance form that is today known as the modern dance.

When the term 'modern dance' was coined about 1927, it well suited the dancers it described, for they believed that dance should reflect contemporary attitudes and preoccupations. Even when they set their works in other periods, as Graham did with her Greek mythological pieces, they drew upon 20th-century insights in evolving their themes. In later years, however, 'modern dance' came to embrace a broad spectrum of principles and techniques, some with goals far removed from those of the original modern dancers. Today the phrase no longer implies a singleminded commitment to the expression of modern life.

Graham, Humphrey and Weidman began by repudiating the glamour and exoticism that had given Denishawn much of its appeal, for they believed that dance should provoke, stimulate and inform rather than simply entertain. They wanted to confront the problems that real people faced – including, in a post-Freudian era, sex. Audiences often found their works ugly and depressing; not for these choreographers were the comforts of escapism. Their interest in the human condition was manifested in different ways: Graham's works usually explored the individual psyche, while Humphrey was fascinated by the interactions of the individual and the group. Weidman is best remembered for his use of humour and satire to point out human foibles.

As part of their effort to strip away what they saw as the decadent and artificial prettiness of both ballet and Denishawn, both Graham and Humphrey searched for the fundamental principles of movement. Both evolved theories that became the bases of their dance techniques. The basic human function of breathing inspired Graham's theory of contraction and release, which grew into a complex network of associations. Contraction,

78 Pearl Primus used West Indian and African dance as the basis for her powerful works on Negro themes.

which curved the chest inwards and rounded the back, caused the dancer to focus on his own centre; it could be used to suggest fear, sorrow, withdrawal or introversion. Release, which expanded the chest by filling the lungs with air, could signify affirmation, acceptance or ecstasy. When used in conjunction, the two movements heightened each other's effect; also, the emotional states they communicated could be subtly varied: a contraction with the head raised could create the effect of a gasp of joy. The principle of contraction and release could also be applied to other parts of the body. As Graham developed her dance technique she added shapes like the spiral (a basic form in nature) to give a more lyrical dimension to her dancing.

Humphrey formulated the theory of fall and recovery, which she called 'the arc between two deaths'. At one extreme lay the complete surrender to gravity; at the other was the achievement of balance and stability. To Humphrey, neither extreme was interesting in itself; rather, the emotional and physical drama of dancing sprang from the dancer's struggle against the forces of gravity and inertia, and his willingness to take the risk of abandoning equilibrium.

Graham led the exodus from Denishawn in 1923, believing that there could be no scope for her ambitions in a company that already boasted St Denis as its established star. Although the works presented on her first independent dance concert in 1926 bore the Denishawn imprint – the solo *Tanagra*, for instance, featured the manipulation of a billowing veil, a favourite Denishawn device – she soon began to develop her own creative voice. Louis Horst (1884–1964), her musical director, served as her mentor during her formative years as a choreographer. He composed music for many of her early works, encouraged her to commission scores from contemporary composers (Samuel Barber, Aaron Copland, Paul Hindemith and Gian Carlo Menotti have all composed scores for her) and introduced her, through photographs, to Wigman's art.

Heretic (1929), her first important group work, portrayed the pitiless rejection of an individual by a group in generalized terms that made it applicable to many situations. It was danced, however, in a stark, percussive style that baffled many viewers. Simple, uncompromising movements – clenched fists, the thud of heels, the formation of a wall of bodies – combined with severe costumes and the dancers' deliberately unglamorous appearance to create a look quite different from Denishawn's exotic spectacles.

Graham's early works were determinedly austere both in movement and costume; she later called this her 'long woolens' period. She designed the costumes herself and did without scenery. The solo *Lamentation* (1930) displays her skill in exploiting the qualities of fabric: the dancer's grief is expressed through the angular lines of tension she creates in the long, tight

79 Martha Graham's early works, among them Primitive Mysteries *(1931), were deliberately austere in choreography, scenery and costume. Graham (in white) played the Virgin, the focus of a ritual of the American Southwest.*

tube of stretch jersey she wears. With the passage of time, however, Graham began to make greater use of scenery, costume and lighting. A frequent collaborator was the Japanese-American designer Isamu Noguchi, whose stylized sets well suited the nonliteral style of her choreography.

Although Graham's repertory is highly varied, two major themes recur in her work. The first is based on the American and Amerindian experience. She choreographed *Primitive Mysteries* (1931) after a visit to the American Southwest, utilizing the region's unique blend of Spanish Christianity and Indian culture in a powerful re-enactment of a ritual in honour of the Virgin Mary. The three sections of the work recall the principal events in Mary's life: the birth of Jesus, his crucifixion, and her own assumption into heaven. The simple, staccato movements emphasize the dancers' connection to the earth; at one point the white-clad soloist, who represents the Virgin, lies on the floor. Graham's exploitation of the force of gravity and her development of floorwork (falling, sitting, lying, kneeling and so on) were diametrically opposed to the ballet's attempts to create an illusion of weightlessness.

In the solo *Frontier* (1935), danced to music by Horst, the woman's conquest of space becomes a metaphor for the courage and determination of America's first settlers. Graham used scenery for the first time in this dance: Noguchi's simple set consists of a section of fence and two ropes arranged in a

80 In a joyous moment from Martha Graham's Appalachian Spring *(1944), the Bride (Graham) and the Husbandman (Erick Hawkins) dance together.*

v-shape that extends upward into infinity. The fence provides a 'home base' for the dancer, whose fearless advance with high kicks and jumps alternates with quieter passages, including one in which she appears to cradle a child.

Graham's early company was entirely female; her first male-female duet appeared in *American Document* (1938), an encapsulation of American history. In the section 'Puritan Episode', which treated the subject of sexual repression, she danced with Erick Hawkins (b. 1909), a former ballet dancer who became her husband, partner and leading male dancer for many years.

Graham's most famous Americana piece, *Appalachian Spring* (1944), is danced to a commissioned score that won a Pulitzer Prize for its composer, Aaron Copland. Though the work is set in the nation's early days, it celebrates domestic values rather than the pioneering spirit of *Frontier*. A husbandman (Hawkins) and his bride (Graham) settle into their new home, which is suggested rather than realistically depicted by Noguchi's stylized house-frame. The youthful exuberance of the young couple (shadowed, however, by the doubts and fears of inexperience), contrasts with the steadiness of a pioneer woman (May O'Donnell), while a revivalist (Merce Cunningham) and his four female followers symbolize the religious conviction upon which the nation was built.

The second major current in Graham's work is Greek mythology, which she first began to draw upon in the 1940s. She uses the myths and the characters in them not for their colour or historical interest (as the Romantic

81 As Jocasta (Martha Graham) and Oedipus (Bertram Ross) unknowingly joined in incestuous love in Graham's Night Journey *(1947), they were bound by a rope that also symbolized the umbilical cord. Their bed, designed by Isamu Noguchi, suggests human bones or an instrument of torture.*

ballet or Denishawn might have), but as icons of human, or more specifically, feminine experience. These works confront emotions that everyone has felt: jealousy, fear, guilt, anxiety, self-doubt.

Cave of the Heart (1946) was originally called *Serpent Heart*, a title keyed to the dominant movement motif of the protagonist, Medea. As in Noverre's *Médée et Jason*, Graham's work focuses on Medea's consuming jealousy, which drives her to kill her lover Jason as well as her rival. Her movements evoke a serpent's sinuosity, its writhings and lashings. In a repeated image she crosses the floor on her knees like a snake crawling on its belly. The serpent metaphor implies that in succumbing to her hatred she has become less than human.

Night Journey (1947) retold another famous Greek myth from the woman's point of view. The work begins as Jocasta contemplates the rope with which she will strangle herself; in a flashback she recalls the triumphal arrival of Oedipus, the ignored warnings of the blind seer Tiresias, her marriage with Oedipus and the final revelation that she is his mother as well as his wife. The duet of the lovers on their bone-like marriage bed (designed by Noguchi)

suggests the dual nature of their relationship: Jocasta's caresses echo a mother's cradling, and the rope that binds them in sexual love also symbolizes the umbilical cord; ultimately it becomes the instrument of Jocasta's destruction.

Although her capacity for lyricism was revealed in *Diversion of Angels* (1948), a celebration of love, and she proved she could be funny in *Every Soul is a Circus* (1939), Graham is best known for works that probe unflinchingly into the darker reaches of the soul. *Letter to the World* (1940), a study of an individual's inner life, was based upon the life and works of Emily Dickinson. The American poet is represented by two performers, a dancer and a dancer-actress who recites excerpts from her poetry. Dickinson's great appetite for life, revealed by her poems, is inhibited and even foiled by the grim Ancestress, a symbol of duty and obligation, perhaps even of death. In the end, however, the poet quietly reaffirms her faith in her art.

Similar in purpose but more innovative in form was *Deaths and Entrances* (1943), which was inspired by the three Brontë sisters. Linear time is completely abandoned; the eldest sister (Graham), revisits the past in a series of flashbacks triggered by objects in a manner reminiscent of the literary techniques of James Joyce and Marcel Proust. Three little girls represent memories of the sisters' childhood. Two principal men, the Dark Beloved (Hawkins) and the Poetic Beloved (Cunningham), may be two aspects of the same person, the eldest sister's lover. Graham contrasted Hawkins's strong, commanding movement style with Cunningham's more mercurial quality to suggest different personality traits.

In 1958 Graham again turned to Greek myth for the evening-long *Clytemnestra*. In this intense, often difficult work, the ill-fated Greek queen, unable to find peace after death, reviews her life in an effort to come to terms with her guilt. In a series of images recalled in stream-of-consciousness fashion, she sees again her sister Helen, whose beauty sparked the Trojan War; her husband Agamemnon, who earned her hatred through his decision to sacrifice their daughter for the war's sake; her ambitious and grasping lover Aegisthus; and her son Orestes, fated to kill her in revenge for her murder of Agamemnon. As the relationship of events becomes clear in Clytemnestra's mind, she arrives at self-understanding. The work unfolds with the timeless quality of a ritual, with emotional revelation as its ultimate goal.

Graham ceased to perform in 1969, but continues to choreograph new works for her company. Her dance technique is taught around the world, and two important dance companies in addition to her own use it as the basis of their choreography. The Batsheva Dance Company was founded in Tel Aviv in 1963, with Graham as its artistic adviser. London Contemporary Dance Theatre was founded in England in 1967 with the American dancer

82 Religious ecstasy and sexual repression both emerged in the ritual dances of The Shakers *(1931), created by Doris Humphrey (centre), who danced the central role of the Eldress.*

Robert Cohan (a former member of the Graham company) as its artistic director. Both companies perform works by Graham as well as pieces by other choreographers.

Humphrey's approach to movement took a somewhat different tack from Graham's. Although she too believed in the bond between movement and emotional expression, which she called moving 'from the inside out', she also made a more objective analysis of the craft of choreography, which was published posthumously in her book *The Art of Making Dances* (1958). She frequently worked with abstractions in the sense that she did not always depict specific characters and events. Her dances were metaphors, however, for human situations. She preferred to demonstrate her ideas in movement terms rather than to sum them up in symbols: for example, she believed that the concept of democracy was more convincingly conveyed by a fugue uniting four different themes than by a woman in red, white and blue.

The new direction that Humphrey's work would take was revealed in the first independent concert that she and Weidman presented after leaving Denishawn in 1928. In *Color Harmony* (1928), a silvery figure (Weidman)

representing the artistic intelligence organizes the mingled colours of the spectrum into a harmonious design. Unlike St Denis's music visualizations, which simply strove to reflect musical structure, Humphrey's choreography always grew out of an underlying idea.

Water Study (1928) was an experiment in discarding what she called the 'cerebral' rhythms of music in favour of the natural phrasing of breathing. Like many of Duncan's dances, it was inspired by the observation of natural phenomena. In a silence broken only by the sounds of their breathing, the kneeling dancers arch their backs to imitate the surging and cresting of waves; rising to their feet, they run together, meeting and falling away from one another like large masses of water crashing and subsiding.

Humphrey's *Drama of Motion* (1930) attempted to establish dance as an independent art by abandoning music and concentrating on formal elements such as design, rhythm and dynamics, which gave rise to the theme. Although she saw this as an antidote to the emoting and 'self-expression' that prevailed in the work of many modern dancers of the time, one of her best-known dances, *The Shakers* (1931), reverted to the portrayal of emotion. It was inspired by the religious practice of the Shakers, a Christian sect that requires its members to be celibate, and evokes their rituals by segregating the sexes and incorporating shaking movements into the choreography. The trembling of the men and women as they meet suggests their sexual repression as well as expressing the idea of being shaken clean of sin.

New Dance Trilogy presented Humphrey's critique of contemporary society and her vision of the future. Although the three works were never performed together, they were united by the continuity of their themes; also, all three were danced to scores by Wallingford Riegger. *Theatre Piece* (1936) depicts contemporary life as a vicious competition among various members of the community – businessmen, working women, athletes, actors – who are all seeking selfish goals. In *With My Red Fires* (1936), two lovers defy a powerful Matriarch who represents the negative aspects of authority. *New Dance* (1935), which was actually created first, portrays an ideal world in which individuals are able to work in harmony with the group without losing their own identities. This idea is presented in pure dance terms: the soloists and ensemble relate harmoniously to each other, and in the 'Variations and Conclusion' individuals step forward to dance brief solos, then melt back into the group.

In the 1940s Humphrey began to work intensively with her former pupil José Limón (1908–72), refining his skills both as a dancer and a choreographer. After her retirement from performing she became the artistic director of his company and created several works for it. *Day on Earth* (1947), danced to music by Copland, is a simple but eloquent allegory of life. The labours of the man (Limón) are interrupted by an idyll with a young girl, his first love. A second woman becomes his wife, and they have a child. After the child leaves to lead her own life, the wife grieves, resumes work for a time, then dies, leaving the man to find solace in labour. At the end the child returns, and the three adults, lying on the ground, pull a cloth over themselves.

Humphrey's dance technique was carried on in a somewhat modified form by Limón and his company. Limón's most famous work, *The Moor's Pavane* (1949), distils the Shakespearean story of Othello. Only four characters appear: Othello (Limón) and his bride, the innocent and trustful Desdemona; the treacherous Iago, whose insinuations about Desdemona's infidelity will ultimately lead Othello to murder her; and Iago's wife Emilia, who becomes his cat's-paw. The action is played out within the framework of a formalized courtly dance, its sense of control contrasting sharply with the strong passions of the characters. In one of the dance's most striking images Iago clings leech-like to the back of the reluctant Othello, pouring venom into his ears.

Weidman's lighter touch provided a welcome relief in the serious, sometimes sombre world of modern dance. A gifted mime, he invented what he called kinetic pantomime, which was less literal and more dance-like than its predecessors. He used spoken texts to accompany his autobiographical works *On My Mother's Side* (1940) and *And Daddy Was a Fireman* (1943) and often culled themes from literary sources. *The Happy Hypocrite* (1931) depicted Max Beerbohm's witty tale of Lord George Hell, a roué who is reformed by donning the mask of a saint. *Candide* (1933) was based on

83 The stately formality of José Limón's The Moor's Pavane *(1949) contrasts with the violent passions of Othello (Limón, far left), who bows to Desdemona (Betty Jones, far right) as the predatory Iago (Lucas Hoving) and Emilia (Pauline Koner) look on.*

Voltaire's satire, while *Fables for Our Time* (1947) captures James Thurber's rueful humour in vignettes such as 'The Unicorn in the Garden', in which a man tries to persuade his wife that he really has seen the mythical beast.

Flickers (1941), one of his best-loved works, is an affectionate parody of silent movie themes. In 'Hearts Aflame', villains armed with a mortgage threaten a farmer and his daughter. The vamp of 'Wages of Sin' infects her love-stricken victim with leprosy, giving him a fit of violent scratching. A devastating sheik, à la Valentino, abducts a flapper in 'Flowers of the Desert'; 'Hearts Courageous' depicts a pioneer family besieged by Indians.

Though famed for his comic works, Weidman also had a serious side. *Lynchtown* (1936) depicted the unthinking savagery of a mob bent on the destruction of its chosen victim; the impact of the piece was not negated by the fact that the violence took place offstage.

Despite the similarity of their goals, a certain rivalry existed between Graham's dancers and the Humphrey-Weidman group. They met on common ground, however, at the Bennington School of the Dance, established by Martha Hill in 1934 at Bennington College in Vermont. These summer workshops and their associated festivals, presented annually until 1942, gave Graham, Humphrey, Weidman, Hanya Holm (head of the Wigman School in New York) and others an opportunity to teach their techniques and choreograph new works. *With My Red Fires, Letter to the World* and *Deaths and Entrances* were all created at Bennington. John Martin of the *New York Times*, the first dance critic appointed by a major American newspaper, taught dance history and criticism, while Horst taught dance composition. Many students were college or university teachers, who disseminated what they had learned all over the country.

Some choreographers went even further than Graham, Humphrey or Weidman in their search for relevance to modern life. Some based their themes on contemporary political events. The high-minded ideals of the Communists inspired Edith Segal's *The Belt Goes Red* (1930), in which an assembly-line of white-clad workers constructs a 'machine' made of dancers in black, then winds it about with a red banner. Segal's company belonged to the Workers' Dance League, a confederation of dance groups founded in 1933 for the purpose of political activism through dance. These groups often performed at political rallies and labour union meetings, for they wanted to bring their messages to new audiences.

Another member of the Workers' Dance League was the New Dance Group, formed in 1934, which both taught and performed. To fulfil its goal of making dance accessible to all, it offered classes for very low tuition fees and based its theatrical pieces on problems of general concern, such as hunger, unemployment and war. Its leaders included three members of Graham's company, Jane Dudley, Sophie Maslow and Anna Sokolow, and a Humphrey–Weidman dancer, William Bales. In the 1940s the group's focus shifted to American folk themes and it began to produce works such as Maslow's *Folksay* (1942), which employs folk songs, a text by Carl Sandburg and a deceptively relaxed style of dancing to recreate the genial tone of life in rural America.

American material was also used by Helen Tamiris (1905–66), whose background lay in ballet and musical comedy. She too shared the ideals of social commitment and wanted to bring dance to a wider audience. She is best known for her *Negro Spirituals*, a series of dances that she choreographed between 1928 and 1942. Different aspects of the black experience in America are expressed in these songs and dances, from the weariness and desolation of 'Nobody Knows the Trouble I See' to the aggressive energy of 'Joshua Fit de Battle ob Jericho'; while the power and yearning of 'Go Down Moses' contrast with the frenetic good cheer of 'Git on Board, Lil' Chillun'.

Tamiris's *How Long Brethren?* (1937), danced to Negro protest songs, was produced by the Federal Dance Project, organized in 1935 by the Works

84, 85 As an irresistible sheik in his silent-movie spoof Flickers *(1941), Charles Weidman literally danced his conquest (Beatrice Seckler) up a wall (right). Katherine Dunham's* Tropical Revue *(left) introduced audiences to a wide variety of black dances, ranging from jazz-dancing to re-creations of primitive rituals such as 'Rara Tonga' (1942), in which she appears here (centre).*

Progress Administration as part of its effort to alleviate the widespread unemployment of the Depression. This marked the first time that public funds were used in the U.S. to create dance works. The Dance Project was most active in New York and Chicago; among its participants were Humphrey, Weidman, Ruth Page and Katherine Dunham.

The early works of Anna Sokolow (b.1912), a member of Graham's company and the New Dance Group, were appeals to the political and social conscience of her audience. *Slaughter of the Innocents* (1937), for instance, was inspired by the Spanish Civil War. Although her works continued to bear on contemporary life, her emphasis shifted in the 1950s to themes of alienation and isolation. The dancers in *Rooms* (1955) seem to be alone even when they are on stage together; they never make eye contact with one another. Their repetitive movements verge on compulsiveness: a man gives way to the jitters; a woman acts out frustrated sexual longings; three women indulge in narcissistic self-absorption; another man flees invisible demons. Sokolow's vision of the 20th century is predominantly dark and pessimistic; she captures the despair of man in his urban jungles.

Lester Horton (1906–53), who did most of his work in California, was initially inspired by Amerindian dances and customs, but expanded his interests to include other cultures. His company, founded in Los Angeles in 1932, was among the first to include black, Hispanic and Asian dancers as well as whites. He evolved a dance technique that incorporated movements adapted from ethnic dance forms and trained the body to move with intricacy and fluidity. A complete man of the theatre, he often composed the music and designed the sets and costumes for his own choreography. His flair for drama is demonstrated in *The Beloved* (1948), a savage tale of a man who murders his wife.

Black dance was recognized in the 1930s and 40s as an art form worthy of serious consideration. The two leading lights of this movement were Katherine Dunham (b.1912) and Pearl Primus (b.1919), both of whom earned doctoral degrees in anthropology and did field work in Africa and the Caribbean. Both were magnetic performers and creative artists as well as scholars, and both used their research as the basis of exciting theatrical pieces.

Like Graham, Dunham had a special interest in ritual, which she used as the theme of several dances. *L'Ag'ya* (1938), first produced by the Federal Dance Project, depicts a love triangle on the island of Martinique. The rival suitors resolve their conflict with a traditional duel in rhythmic form, accompanied by singing and drumming. *Rites of Passage* (1941) recreates a young man's initiation into adulthood and the courtship of a young couple. Dunham's lively, colourfully costumed works, presented in popular programmes such as her *Tropical Revue* of 1943, introduced black dance to many new audiences.

She also developed her own technique, which is based on the isolation of body parts (that is, the movement of different parts of the body independently of the others), a characteristic of many African dance forms.

Primus, who made her debut as a dancer in 1943, developed a less *78* glamorous performing image than Dunham. Her powerful dances are often inspired by the vicissitudes of black Americans: *Hard Time Blues* (1943), for example, protested against the gruelling life of sharecroppers. Like Dunham, she has re-created African and Caribbean dances and rituals in works such as *Fanga* (1949), a West African greeting dance.

La Meri (Russell Meriwether Hughes, b.1898) studied and performed ethnic dances in Asia, Africa, Spain and Latin America. She strove to make her dances as accurate and authentic as possible, although she understood that some nuances could only be captured by a native. Her research was published in *The Gesture Language of the Hindu Dance* (1941) and *Spanish Dancing* (1948). In 1940 she and St Denis opened the School of Natya (Hindu dance) in New York City; this was later absorbed into her Ethnologic Dance Center, which operated from 1942 to 1956. One of her most successful dances was a translation of *Swan Lake* into Hindu dance movements, choreographed in 1944. She retained the ballet's music and plot, but added a prologue explaining how the Hamsa Rani (Swan Queen) was enchanted, and a danced fight between the Prince and the Enchanter.

The efforts of Dunham, Primus and La Meri helped establish the artistic value and integrity of ethnic dance. By demonstrating the richness of authentic forms, they encouraged other dancers and audiences to view and study ethnic dances with new respect.

Modern dance of the 1930s and 40s truly lived up to its name. It embodied many of the complexities and contradictions of the modern world. It was forward-looking and propounded visions of the ideal society with a crusader's zeal, but it could also be introspective, intensely personal and engrossed with the past. It confronted the grim realities of life, but also found places for lyricism and humour. It sought to express the American heritage, yet it also recognized the ethnic diversity of Americans and tried to convey this too through dance. Despite the diversity of its characteristics and purposes, however, modern dance was unified by its emphasis on the expression of feelings through dance, as opposed to a purely decorative display of technique.

Perhaps the term 'modern dance' has persisted because of its close association with the idea of innovation. Certainly the 1930s and 40s introduced new ways of moving, new subject matter and new ways to express an idea or structure a narrative. These innovations provided the groundwork for future achievements both in modern dance and in ballet.

CHAPTER NINE

The Decentralization of Ballet

With the deaths of Diaghilev in 1929 and Pavlova in 1931, the Russian monopoly on western ballet began to weaken. Although the tradition of the Ballets Russes was carried on, new ballet companies with strong national identities sprang up in Britain, France and the U.S. in the 1930s and 40s. To some extent, however, all had the Russian ballet tradition behind them. Marie Rambert and Ninette de Valois, the founders of the two major British ballet companies, were former members of the Diaghilev ballet, as were Alicia Markova and Anton Dolin, the two foremost British dancers of the period. The Paris Opéra Ballet, which had fallen into decline in the late 19th century, was given new strength and purpose by Serge Lifar, Diaghilev's last male star. In the U.S., Balanchine sought to develop an American style of ballet grounded on the vocabulary and discipline of the Russian tradition.

Diaghilev's company, which was disbanded at his death, had been the lodestar of western ballet for twenty years, and its name and heritage were eventually claimed by two rival companies. The first made its debut in 1932 as the Ballets Russes de Monte-Carlo. It subsequently appeared under several different names, including the Original Ballet Russe, but for the sake of convenience it will be called here the de Basil Ballets Russes after its director Colonel Wassily de Basil (1888–1951). The second, best known as the Ballet Russe de Monte Carlo, was directed by Sergei Denham and gave its first performance in 1938.

There was a great deal of crossover of personnel between the two companies: Massine, Nijinska and Balanchine choreographed new ballets for both, and dancers such as Markova, Lifar, Alexandra Danilova (b.1904), André Eglevsky and Igor Youskevitch appeared with both companies. The repertories of both centred upon favourite ballets from the Diaghilev era, such as Fokine's *Les Sylphides*, *Petrouchka* and *Schéhérazade*; Nijinsky's *L'Après-midi d'un faune*; and Massine's *Le Tricorne*.

Balanchine, de Basil's first resident choreographer, engaged three phenomenally talented teenagers who became popularly known as the 'baby ballerinas'. Irina Baronova (b.1919) and Tamara Toumanova (b.1919) were thirteen, and Tatiana Riabouchinska (b.1917) was sixteen. Toumanova created the role of the Young Girl in Balanchine's *Cotillon* (1932), a lighthearted picture of young people at a ball. An air of mystery entered this

86 Serge Lifar in Icare *(1935), which tells the story of Icarus's ill-fated attempt to fly. Lifar took an experimental approach to the ballet's music: there was no attempt to fit the choreography to a score; instead, percussion instruments performed rhythms that had been composed to follow the dancer's movements.*

ballet with the 'Hand of Fate' pas de deux, in which a man encounters a vampiric black-gloved woman.

When Balanchine left in 1933, Massine took his place. His ballets for de Basil did not differ much in essence from those he later choreographed for Denham's Ballet Russe de Monte Carlo. Critics classified his ballets into two major types: character ballets, continuing the vein of *La Boutique Fantasque* and *Le Tricorne*, and symphonic ballets. Into the first category fell *Le Beau Danube* (de Basil, 1933) and *Gaité Parisienne* (Denham, 1938), both frothy romances that showed off the talents of the glamorous Danilova. As the worldly street dancer in *Le Beau Danube* she danced a nostalgic waltz with her former lover, a dashing hussar (Massine). *Gaité*, which was particularly adored by audiences of its time, featured her as a glove-seller in love with a baron (Frederic Franklin, her longtime partner). Massine played an eccentric Peruvian, agog at the delights of Paris. The whole was topped off by a sparkling medley of tunes from Offenbach's operettas.

Similar in nature was *Union Pacific* (de Basil, 1934), which some critics derided as unconvincing: America seen through Russian eyes. Based on a historical event, the competition of Irish and Chinese labourers to complete the Union Pacific railroad, it contained witty characterizations such as the high-class courtesan Lady Gay (Eugenia Delarova) and Massine's own Barman. Toumanova performed a Mexican hat dance on pointe.

Massine's symphonic ballets, a noble if not entirely successful experiment, resembled Lopukhov's *Tanzsynfonia* in their use of symphonic music by great composers. Massine generally gave these ballets large-scale themes based on abstract qualities such as love and adversity. An exception was *Symphonie Fantastique* (de Basil, 1936), in which he followed the scenario devised by the composer, Hector Berlioz: under the influence of opium, a young musician dreams of his elusive beloved, who finally appears to him as a witch at a black sabbath. The symphonic ballets were considered highly controversial, for many people still disapproved of the use of 'great music' for dance. Symphonic music, they felt, was complete in itself and needed no illustration by dance.

Massine's ingenious handling of groups, a highly praised facet of his symphonic ballets, benefited from his interchange with the dancer Nina Verchinina, who had studied Laban's method and provided a link with Central European modern dance. She created the role of Action in his first symphonic ballet, *Les Présages* (de Basil, 1933), danced to Tchaikovsky's Fifth Symphony, an allegory of man's struggle against destiny. Baronova and Riabouchinska were acclaimed in the respective roles of Passion and Frivolity. Verchinina also led the sombre second movement of *Choreartium* (de Basil, 1933), which relied less on symbolism, though it strove to reflect

87, 88 Massine's works are usually grouped into character ballets, such as Gaité Parisienne *(left) and symphonic ballets such as* Les Présages *(right). Alexandra Danilova's glamour and ebullience helped make* Gaité Parisienne *a great popular success; she was partnered by the British dancer Frederic Franklin. In the abstract world of* Les Présages *the 'baby ballerina' Irina Baronova, seen here in the arms of Fate, represented Passion.*

the varying moods of Brahms's Fourth Symphony. For Denham's company Massine choreographed Beethoven's Seventh Symphony (1938), which was criticized for the second movement's allusions to the crucifixion of Christ, and *Rouge et Noir* (1939), to Shostakovitch's First Symphony, in which the colours of the dancers' costumes were assigned allegorical meanings.

Bacchanale (Denham, 1939) defied categorization. It was a foray into 89 surrealism, aided by the designs of Salvador Dali. Danced to the Venusberg music from Wagner's *Tannhäuser*, the ballet portrayed the fantasies of the mad King Ludwig II of Bavaria. The cast included a fish-headed woman; the Knight of Death, conceived of as a dancing umbrella; and the historical figure of Leopold von Sacher-Masoch, who gratefully receives physical abuse from his wife.

89 Among the surrealistic surprises of Massine's Bacchanale *(1939), designed by Salvador Dali, was a dancer with a fish's head. The ballet, danced to music from Wagner's* Tannhäuser*, depicts the hallucinations of the mad Ludwig II.*

After Massine's departure Fokine joined de Basil's company, refurbishing his existing works and creating a few new ones, among them *Paganini* (1939), inspired by the legendary violinist. The dancer David Lichine (1910–72) created one of the company's most popular works, *Graduation Ball* (1940), in which finishing-school girls and cadets from a military academy meet with all the attendant ecstasies and embarrassments.

After the summer of 1938, when the rivals played concurrent seasons in London, the two Ballet Russe companies each established its own territory. Denham's Ballet Russe de Monte Carlo toured the U.S. and Canada, while de Basil's company danced in Europe, Australia and Latin America. Both companies strove to maintain a Russian mystique, initially justified by their cores of Russian and Polish dancers from the Diaghilev company. As time went by, however, both companies employed many British, American, Canadian and Australian dancers, who initially tried to conceal their true nationalities under Russianized stage names.

One of the most successful ballets mounted by the Ballet Russe de Monte Carlo was the work of an American choreographer, Agnes de Mille (b. 1909). *Rodeo* (1942), danced to a score by Copland, told the story of a cowgirl who tries in vain to emulate the cowboys' feats, but at last puts on a dress and wins her man. *Rodeo* abandoned the ballet dancer's traditional aristocratic bearing

90 An all-American square dance, accompanied by hand-clapping and a caller, provides a transitional scene in Agnes de Mille's Rodeo *(1942).*

in favour of a more informal type of movement that better suited the characters portrayed. The cowboys engage in bronco-busting and lariat-twirling; the girls flirt, gossip and surreptitiously adjust their stockings and girdles. Local colour was supplied by a rousing square dance, complete with caller. De Mille made these movements into dance, stretching the boundaries of the acceptable in ballet much as Balanchine had in *Apollon Musagète*.

Balanchine himself served as resident choreographer of the Ballet Russe de Monte Carlo between 1944 and 1946, and helped revitalize the company at a time when its creative powers were flagging. Among his new works for the company were *Danses Concertantes* (1944), a pure dance piece to music by Stravinsky, and *Night Shadow* (1946), later revived under the title *La Sonnambula*, the haunting tale of a poet who falls in love with a mysterious and alluring sleepwalker.

After his resignation, several American choreographers contributed to the repertory. Among them was Valerie Bettis (b. 1920), the first modern dancer

to work for a ballet company. Her *Virginia Sampler* (1947) was a divertissement depicting the early days of the state of Virginia; however, the dancers could not assimilate her style, and the ballet did not succeed. Ruth Page (b.1900) restaged the popular *Frankie and Johnny*, which she had created in collaboration with Bentley Stone in 1938. An ironic tale of a prostitute who murders her pimp, it was accompanied by four female singers in Salvation Army uniforms. Ruthanna Boris's pas de deux *Cirque de Deux* (1947) humorously satirized the pretensions of classical ballet dancers.

In contrast to the Ballet Russe companies, with their cosmopolitan rosters and perennial touring, several companies began to develop a national identity. In England Marie Rambert (1888–1982) and her students began to present small-scale ballet productions in the mid 1920s, including the first ballet by Frederick Ashton (b.1904), *A Tragedy of Fashion* (1926). This group eventually grew into a professional company, Ballet Rambert. Ninette de Valois (b.1898), who dreamed of establishing a British ballet company, opened a school in London in 1926. With the support of Lilian Baylis, the manager of the Old Vic Theatre, she formed the company that came to be known as the Sadler's Wells Ballet.

Both of these companies benefited from the backing of the Camargo Society, organized in 1930 by the critics Arnold Haskell and Philip J. S. Richardson. It was not itself a company; its quarterly productions, presented before a subscription audience, drew dancers from both Rambert's and de Valois's groups. Its governing committee included the economist John Maynard Keynes, his ballerina wife Lydia Lopokova, the composers Edwin Evans and Constant Lambert, and Rambert and de Valois.

The Camargo Society provided support for British ballet at a crucial period in its growth. It allowed the fledgling companies to mount productions on a larger scale than either could afford alone, and encouraged budding British choreographers such as Frederick Ashton to work with eminent composers and designers. Dancers of the highest calibre were engaged as guest artists, among them Dolin, Lopokova, Markova and Spessivtseva.

The society's most notable productions were Ashton's *Façade* and de Valois's *Job* (both 1931). *Façade* was danced to music by William Walton and poems by Edith Sitwell that had originally been composed as an 'entertainment' for the Sitwell family. Intended as a parody of popular dances, it included a 'Yodelling Song' for Lopokova as a milkmaid, a 'Polka' danced by Markova in a brief costume and a 'Tango Pasadoble' in which Ashton played an insinuating Latin lover with Lopokova as his shrinking inamorata. *Job* was cast in quite a different mould: it was based on the biblical story of the trials of Job as visualized by William Blake, whose illustrations inspired the ballet's designs by Gwen Raverat. Dolin played the spectacular role of Satan, who at one point rolled headlong down the steps that symbolically separated heaven and earth. The score was composed by Ralph Vaughan Williams.

The Camargo Society was dissolved in 1934, leaving its ballets to de Valois's company, which was on a more secure financial footing than Rambert's. However, Rambert's classes and Sunday night performances continued to foster the talents of many budding dancers and choreographers. One of her most famous pupils was Antony Tudor (1908–87), whose best-known ballet, *Jardin aux Lilas* [*Lilac Garden*] (1936), was created for the Ballet 92 Rambert. This ballet first revealed his ability to express psychological nuance through movement. The scene is a garden party celebrating the betrothal of the heroine, Caroline, to a man she does not love. Among the guests are her lover and her fiancé's former mistress. The emotional turmoil of the quartet is conveyed through expressive gestures (a hand to the brow, a restless rise onto pointe) knit into the fabric of the academic ballet vocabulary. As the music rises to a climax the action freezes, and Caroline moves gropingly among the still figures as though seeking to escape. But she does not succeed, and her fiancé reclaims her.

Although Tudor danced briefly with the Sadler's Wells Ballet, the company's limited budget did not permit him to choreograph a ballet for it. He left to form his own company, and in 1940 emigrated to the U.S. to join the newly organized Ballet Theatre. De Valois and Ashton, the principal choreographers of Sadler's Wells, thus became the primary shapers of British ballet. With Markova as their first prima ballerina they began to build a repertory based on classics such as *Swan Lake* and *Giselle*, leavened with new works.

91 Frederick Ashton's first ballet, A Tragedy of Fashion *(1926), wittily depicted the trials and tribulations of a couturier, danced by Ashton, who is seen here partnering Marie Rambert as one of his mannequins.*

92 Antony Tudor's Jardin aux Lilas *(1936): on the verge of their marriage of convenience, Caroline and her fiancé (Maude Lloyd and Antony Tudor, centre) cannot suppress lingering regrets for their former loves (Hugh Laing, far left, and Peggy Van Praagh, far right).*

De Valois's most successful ballet of this period was *The Rake's Progress* (1935), which brought to life William Hogarth's series of paintings in which a dissipated man squanders his wealth in gambling and merrymaking, lands in debtors' prison and dies in a madhouse. The British dancer Walter Gore played the rake, with Markova as the girl he has betrayed. The sets and costumes were adapted from Hogarth's paintings by the British artist Rex Whistler.

When Markova departed in 1935, the very young Margot Fonteyn (b.1919) stepped into her roles. In the ensuing years she became Ashton's muse and created leading roles in many of his ballets. Their earliest joint triumph was *Apparitions* (1936), a lushly Romantic work revolving around a poet who is beglamoured by visions of an unattainable woman. Cecil Beaton, whose photographs for *Vogue* had securely established him in the fashionable world, designed the sets and costumes. The poet was played by a young Australian dancer, Robert Helpmann (1909–86), who became renowned for his dramatic ability.

Apparitions was followed by *A Wedding Bouquet* (1937), accompanied by a spoken text by the American writer Gertrude Stein. Ashton's wittily delineated characters included the punctilious housemaid Webster (de Valois), the oily bridegroom (Helpmann) and his demented former love Julia (Fonteyn), whose little dog Pepe (Julia Farron) was inspired by Stein's real Mexican terrier.

Helpmann choreographed *Hamlet* (1942), which presented the events in Shakespeare's play in the form of a flashback introduced by Hamlet's death. The characters appear to be Hamlet's hallucinations; in this Freudian interpretation of the play, the nubile Ophelia (Fonteyn) is often confused with Hamlet's mother, Gertrude. Helpmann's talent as an actor made him an ideal interpreter of the title role.

By 1946 the Sadler's Wells Ballet had gained enough prestige to be invited to reopen the Royal Opera House at Covent Garden, which had been used as a dance-hall during World War II. In honour of the occasion the company mounted a new production of Petipa's *The Sleeping Beauty* (which it had first presented in 1939) with scenery and costumes by the British designer Oliver Messel. Fonteyn and Helpmann danced the leading roles, and Ashton and de

93, 94 Two great British ballets of the 1940s: left, Robert Helpmann's Hamlet *(1942) emphasized the Freudian implications of the drama, particularly in the relationship between Hamlet (Helpmann) and his mother, Gertrude (Celia Franca); right, Ashton's* Symphonic Variations *(1946) starred Margot Fonteyn; it is a plotless ballet that must be danced with absolute classical purity.*

Valois provided additional choreography. The ballet became a signature work of the company and is still closely associated with it.

Ashton's masterly plotless ballet to César Franck's *Symphonic Variations* was also created in 1946. A work of deceptive simplicity, it requires the utmost technical purity from its six dancers, who must maintain a demeanour of unruffled serenity. The cast was headed by Fonteyn and Michael Somes (b.1917), who partnered her for many years.

Across the Channel, the Paris Opéra Ballet was revitalized by Lifar, who became its balletmaster in 1929. At his peak as a dancer in the 1930s, he helped restore the male dancer to a position of importance at the Opéra. His new production of *Giselle* (1932) expanded the role of Albrecht to give it equal importance with that of Giselle, who was played by Olga Spessivtseva, one of the role's greatest interpreters. Lifar also had innovative ideas about choreography, which he described in his *Manifeste du choréographe* (1935). *Icare* (1935) demonstrated his theory that dance should derive from its own rhythms rather than follow those imposed upon it by music. To achieve this, he choreographed the dance first, and the composer J.-E. Szyfer used its rhythms as the foundation of his score. The ballet's story was based on the ancient Greek myth of Icarus (Lifar), whose father Daedalus builds him a pair of artificial wings. Disobeying his father's orders, Icarus flies too close to the sun, which melts the wax in his wings and causes him to plunge to his death.

Finding the Opéra too restrictive, the young French choreographer Roland Petit (b.1924) broke away to form first the Ballets des Champs-Élysées (1945) and later the Ballets de Paris (1948). His ballets, which often blended jazz dancing with classical technique, were known for their chic and sophistication as well as for their sense of drama. *Le Jeune homme et la mort* (1946), conceived by Cocteau, was considered shocking in its day for its juxtaposition of Bach's noble *Passacaglia in C Minor* with the unsavoury story of a young artist who hangs himself in his garret after an acrid encounter with his girlfriend. She returns, masked, as the personification of death. The ballet was actually rehearsed to jazz music, and the Bach score was not used until the dress rehearsal. Jean Babilée (b.1923) was highly praised in the role of the artist. The title role of Petit's *Carmen* (1949), a ballet version of Georges Bizet's opera, is indelibly associated with Petit's wife Renée (Zizi) Jeanmaire (b.1924), whose short hair and long legs gave a radical new look to the operatic heroine. The ballet, which emphasized the sex and violence of the story, included a prolonged bedroom scene for Carmen and her unlucky lover Don José (Petit).

Although ballet in Europe had a strong tendency towards drama, American ballet began to explore a different path due to the influence of Balanchine, who came to the U.S. in 1933 at the invitation of Lincoln

95 The Sleeping Beauty, *which later became a signature work of the Sadler's Wells Ballet, was first produced by the company in 1939. Margot Fonteyn (centre), whose radiant Princess Aurora set a standard for coming generations, is seen here in a moment from the 'Rose Adagio'.*

Kirstein, a scholar and patron of the arts who became his foremost supporter. Recognizing the need for good dance training, Balanchine established the School of American Ballet, which became the main source of dancers for his successive companies: the American Ballet, American Ballet Caravan, Ballet Society and the New York City Ballet (the last, founded in 1948, continues to function today).

Balanchine's work in America reveals an enormous diversity. He mounted new versions of the classics, notably a one-act version of *Swan Lake* (1951) and *The Nutcracker* (1954); traditional story ballets such as *A Midsummer Night's Dream* (1962); and opulent spectacles such as *Vienna Waltzes* (1977). He is best known, however, for his plotless neoclassical ballets, many of which are danced in simple leotards and tights, without scenery, as though to

96, 97 Balanchine ballets of the 1930s: left, Les Ballets 1933 in The Seven Deadly Sins, *danced to music by Kurt Weill, in which the double role of the hapless heroine Anna was shared by the dancer Tilly Losch (left) and the singer Lotte Lenya;* right, *in the first performances of* Serenade *(1935) the women wore short tunics rather than the long blue tutus seen in revivals today, but this pose, here executed by Heidi Vosseler (foreground), Charles Laskey and Elena de Rivas, has not changed.*

dispense with anything that might distract the viewer from the dancing. Among the most famous ballets of this genre are *Concerto Barocco* (1941), which was originally danced in costumes suggesting baroque ornamentation; *The Four Temperaments* (1946); *Agon* (1957); and *Episodes* (1959).

For Balanchine music was the prime motivation for dancing – he called it the floor for dancing – and he used its elements (rhythm, phrasing, texture) to spark his choreographic ideas. He did not, however, superimpose symbolic or dramatic programmes upon it as Massine did in his symphonic ballets, and his choreography reflects the musical structure without attempting to mimic its every turn. He continued to work with Stravinsky, and their collaboration produced ballets such as *Orpheus* (1948), a retelling of the ancient Greek myth, and the plotless *Agon*, both of which were intended to form a 'Greek trilogy' with *Apollo*.

98 Among the masterworks produced by Balanchine in collaboration with Stravinsky was Agon, *a plotless ballet choreographed for the New York City Ballet in 1957. Suzanne Farrell and Peter Martins are the central couple in this photograph of a later performance.*

Serenade (American Ballet, 1935), the first ballet he choreographed on American soil, demonstrates how formal values may coexist with emotional qualities in his work. Most of the ballet (danced to Tchaikovsky's *Serenade in C for string orchestra*) can be viewed as pure dance, but in the concluding 'Elegy', the outlines of a story begin to take shape without ever crystallizing into specific characters or incidents. A girl falls to the floor and is approached by a man whose eyes are covered by a second girl, walking closely behind him. He raises the fallen girl, and they dance together. Then she resumes her original position; the man's eyes are covered once more and he is guided away. The girl, lifted high by three men, is borne away by a cortège-like group.

The Four Temperaments (Ballet Society, 1946) similarly contains emotional resonances that never quite solidify into explicit characterizations. Paul Hindemith's score and the four contrasting sections of the ballet (preceded by three pas de deux danced to variations of the musical theme) evoke the different personalities set forth by the ancient theory of the four temperaments. The slow, weighty movements of the man who dances the Melancholic solo suggest a morose disposition; the Sanguinic couple is more vivacious, executing quick, bright steps. The loose, seemingly purposeless quality of the Phlegmatic man's solo suggests calm indolence, while the Choleric woman attacks the air with high kicks and furiously circling arms.

Although Balanchine's choreography and dancers were considered cold and mechanical well into the 1960s, tastes began to swerve in his favour, and by the time of his death in 1983 he was acknowledged as a master. His impact on American ballet has been so great that a host of imitators has risen in his wake, and many young choreographers have found it difficult to escape his pervasive influence.

Ballet Theatre's approach was quite different, as its very name implies; like its European counterparts, it emphasized the dramatic component of ballet. The company, which gave its first performance in 1940, was organized by the dancer Lucia Chase (1897–1986) and Richard Pleasant (1906–61), who became its first manager. They wanted a company that would be versatile and varied rather than subordinate to a single artistic vision, and to this end they invited many different choreographers to contribute to the repertory. Ashton, Balanchine, de Mille, Dolin, Fokine, Massine, Nijinska and Tudor have all created ballets for the company.

One of the company's first American works was Eugene Loring's *Billy the Kid*. Originally created in 1938 for Ballet Caravan, a company founded by Lincoln Kirstein as a showcase for American talent, *Billy* is a fairy tale of the Wild West. The outlaw William Bonney is portrayed as a sympathetic figure: he is motivated to turn criminal by the accidental murder of his

99 In Tudor's Pillar of Fire *(1942), Nora Kaye (second from right) created a powerful portrait of a sexually repressed woman. The other characters included (left to right) Annabelle Lyon as her younger sister, Tudor as her suitor, Lucia Chase as her elder sister and Hugh Laing as her seducer.*

100 The young outlaw Billy the Kid (Fred Danieli, centre) rejects the offered friendship of Sheriff Pat Garrett (Lew Christensen, left) in a scene from Eugene Loring's Billy the Kid *(1938).*

mother, and his victims are always played by the same man in different guises, who represents his nemesis. Loring's choreography stylized real movements such as horseback riding and playing cards, and included naturalistic touches such as the real cigarette that Billy lights shortly before his death. However, his Mexican sweetheart, who appears to him in a dream, dances on pointe. Steeped in symbolism and romance (the ballet opens and closes with a march representing the westward movement of the pioneers), *Billy* seems remote in contrast with the warmth and immediacy of de Mille's *Rodeo*, acquired by Ballet Theatre in 1950, which makes us recall real people.

The recruitment of Tudor was arguably one of Ballet Theatre's greatest achievements, for he has devoted most of his career to the company, continuing to develop the expression of psychological nuances in ballet. *Pillar of Fire* (1942) was a study of sexual repression. The lonely and unattractive Hagar (Nora Kaye), snatches at a loveless affair only to find guilt and remorse; at last, however, she is redeemed by true love. As in Tudor's *Jardin aux Lilas* (staged for Ballet Theatre in 1940), states of mind or even character traits are suggested by gestures, such as the way in which Hagar tugs at the suffocatingly high collar of her dress, or her straitlaced elder sister pulls her skirts close to her.

147

A sunnier vision of the world was presented by the young American choreographer Jerome Robbins (b. 1918) in *Fancy Free* (1944), a buoyant tale of three sailors on shore leave. The trio behave very little like ballet princes: they chew gum and down mugs of beer with more gusto than grace. They hold a dance competition to see who will win the two girls they have met. The first sailor (Harold Lang) is brashly acrobatic, tossing off splits, jumps and turns; the second (John Kriza) is dreamy and romantic; the third (Robbins) sways his hips to the sexy beat of a rumba. The contest ends in a fight, and the girls hastily flee. Calling a truce, the sailors pledge their friendship – until another girl saunters by. Robbins' mixture of ballet, jazz, and realistic movement was not only convincing but endearing, so much so that he and Leonard Bernstein, the composer, expanded the ballet into a highly successful musical comedy, *On the Town* (1945). *Fancy Free* has the ring of truth, and although the women's fashions place it firmly in the wartime years when it was created, it still looks fresh today. Like de Mille's *Rodeo*, *Fancy Free* helped expand the range of movement that could be accepted in a 'serious' ballet, as opposed to a musical comedy or revue.

Although Ballet Theatre and most of its counterparts were established in large urban areas, a few high-calibre companies were formed in smaller cities. The San Francisco Ballet, which grew up under the directorship of the Christensen brothers (Willam, b. 1902, was appointed in 1938; Lew, 1909–84, a former Balanchine dancer, took over in 1952), presented the first full-length version of *Swan Lake* in the U.S. in 1940. A Canadian company that started in 1938 on a semi-professional basis became in 1953 the first ballet company to receive a royal charter, the Royal Winnipeg Ballet.

For many dancers and choreographers of this period, however, employment opportunities were few and far between. The major ballet and modern dance companies were still at an embryonic stage. Musical comedies and films became important performing outlets, providing not only experience but financial rewards. Although some people disdained these outlets for their commercialism and considered them inferior to the pursuit of serious art, the interaction of the two spheres ultimately resulted in gains for both sides. The influx of ballet and modern choreographers into the musical theatre demanded a higher level of proficiency from the dancers and resulted in choreography more complex than the precision dancing and 'routines' of earlier years. Dance acquired more importance in the general scheme of the musical play. The choreographers benefited in turn, for their works were introduced to a wider audience, and they learned how to expand their appeal.

Among the choreographers who worked for the musical theatre or films were Balanchine, de Mille, Fokine, Holm, Horton, Humphrey, Tamiris, Robbins and Weidman. Several won awards for their work: Tamiris

101 Three insouciant sailors (left to right, Jerome Robbins, John Kriza, Michael Kidd) enjoy a night on the town in Robbins's Fancy Free (1944).

102 The 'Slaughter on Tenth Avenue' ballet that Balanchine created for the musical On Your Toes (1936) was conceived as an integral part of the plot. Here the Strip Tease Girl (Tamara Geva) watches as her lover, the Hoofer (Ray Bolger), fends off a gangster (George Church).

103 *Agnes de Mille's dream ballet in the musical* Oklahoma! *(1943) advanced the plot by clarifying the feelings of the heroine, Laurey (Claire Pasch), towards her suitor Curley (Philip Cook).*

104 *Debonair in top hat and tails, Fred Astaire is still the epitome of masculine grace and elegance to dance lovers all over the world. These photographs show him in* Top Hat *(1935).*

received an Antoinette Perry Award ('Tony') for *Touch and Go* (1949), while Holm won the New York Drama Critics Award for *Kiss Me, Kate* (1948), which became the first choreographic work to be copyrighted by the Library of Congress. The film version of *West Side Story* (1962), which Robbins directed and choreographed, earned him two Academy Awards.

Balanchine introduced the use of the word choreography to Broadway in *On Your Toes* (1936). Unlike most earlier dances in musicals, which existed as separate 'production numbers', his ballets were integrated with the plot, which depicted a music professor's entry into the hothouse world of Russian ballet. The 'Princess Zenobia' ballet was a satire of *Schéhérazade*; 'Slaughter on Tenth Avenue' combined ballet and tap dancing in a tale of doomed love between a hoofer and a stripper. De Mille's history-making dream ballet in *Oklahoma!* (1943), 'Laurey Makes Up Her Mind', advanced the plot by communicating the heroine's doubts and perplexity about which man to choose to take her to a social. Holm had a knack for making dance arise seamlessly out of the action of the play; it never seemed contrived. In 'Another Op'nin', Another Show', which opened *Kiss Me, Kate*, actors and dancers are seen backstage, warming up, practising their parts and releasing high spirits by cavorting as they prepare for a performance.

The British film *The Red Shoes* (1948) stimulated interest in ballet on both sides of the Atlantic. Its title ballet, choreographed by Helpmann, was conceived first, and a somewhat melodramatic story was written around it. The two parallel one another: in Andersen's fairy tale *The Red Shoes*, a girl is punished for dancing instead of going to church, while in the drama a ballerina (Moira Shearer) commits suicide because she cannot decide between her career and marriage. The ballet utilized many cinematic tricks: the red shoes offered to the girl by the sinister shoemaker (Massine) pop magically onto her feet; a drifting sheet of newspaper becomes a male dancer; the ballerina falls weightlessly through space.

Fred Astaire's (1899–1987) unique blend of tap, ballet and ballroom techniques is still studied, through his films, by dancers and choreographers today. The elegance of his dancing recalls the traditions of ballet, yet the characters he played were reassuringly likeable and ordinary despite their extraordinarily nimble feet. In the films he made with Ginger Rogers (b.1911) in the 1930s, dance often helps advance the plot: in the 'Night and Day' duet in *The Gay Divorcee* (1934), for instance, he seductively overcomes Rogers's doubts about him. However, some of the dances within these films are presented as a show-within-the-show, such as 'Let's Face the Music and

Dance', a mini-drama about two unlucky gamblers at Monte Carlo, in *Follow the Fleet* (1936).

The athletically all-American Gene Kelly (b.1912) also combined ballet, tap, jazz, ballroom and gymnastics in his musicals and films, which he often choreographed and directed as well as performed. Dance is well-balanced with drama in his best works and often helps illuminate dramatic situations. In the title ballet of the film *An American in Paris* (1951), danced to George Gershwin's symphonic poem, Kelly's character dreams of pursuing his lost love through an imaginary Paris as seen through the eyes of the painters Vincent Van Gogh, Raoul Dufy, Henri de Toulouse-Lautrec and others. *Singin' in the Rain* (1952), a love story set against the background of Hollywood's effort to introduce talking movies, demonstrates Kelly's knack of opening up dancing spaces in film: 'Good Morning' follows the dancers from room to room, while in the title song Kelly joyously dances down the length of a rain-drenched street.

Soviet Russia aimed for sterner goals. The two major ballet companies, which acquired in this period their present-day names of the Kirov and Bolshoi Ballets (located in Leningrad and Moscow respectively), encouraged a predilection towards drama, which was used in the 1920s and 30s for political purposes. Some ballets were frankly propagandistic. *The Red Poppy* (Bolshoi, 1927) was one of the first examples of this genre. Set in a port in contemporary China, its heroine is a beautiful Chinese dancer who falls in love with a Soviet ship's captain upon observing his attempts to relieve the suffering of the coolies. When her jealous manager tries to murder him, she intercepts the blow and dies. The choreography was a cooperative effort and included contributions by Yekaterina Geltser, who danced the leading role.

Gradually, however, choreographers began to return to ballets of less explicit political content, though most works retained a clear-cut moral. Rostislav Zakharov's ballet *The Fountain of Bakchisarai* (Bolshoi, 1934) was based on a poem by Pushkin. The Khan Girei kidnaps an aristocratic Polish girl, Maria (Galina Ulanova), whose lover he has murdered in a raid on a castle. Maria is killed in turn by Girei's former favourite, but instead of consoling himself with his other wives or finding forgetfulness in battle, he mourns beside a fountain erected in Maria's memory: a savage man ennobled by love.

Ulanova (b.1910), whose artistry made her the best-known Soviet ballerina of her time, considered this ballet a turning point in her career, for she then began to apply Konstantin Stanislavsky's method to her roles, analysing them in depth and detail. The passionate conviction she brought to the role of Juliet in Leonid Lavrovsky's *Romeo and Juliet* (Kirov, 1940) caused her to be identified with the role. Lavrovsky's version of the ballet, first seen

105 The Soviet ballerina Galina Ulanova played the beautiful but pathetic Maria, loved in vain by Khan Girei (Pyotr Gusev), in Rostislav Zakharov's The Fountain of Bakchisarai *(1934).*

in the west as a film, became famous for the strong acting of everyone in its large cast, although some viewers found it choreographically unsatisfying. Prokofiev's score won wider acceptance and has been used for many different versions of this ballet.

By the 1950s ballet was well on its way to becoming a truly international art. No one city could claim to be the centre of the dance world as Paris had been in the Romantic era or St Petersburg in Petipa's heyday. Activity was now more diffuse. Dancers and choreographers no longer had to mask their true nationalities under Russian names; on the contrary, they took pride in expressing their national heritage through dance. Opportunities were growing: the foundations of several major dance companies had been laid, and well-trained dancers were also in demand in musical comedies and films. A period of expansion had begun. No longer was there a single dominating concept of what ballet should be. Each choreographer had his own ideas, as well as his own followers and detractors. Each contributed his own vision to the increasingly kaleidoscopic world of dance.

CHAPTER TEN

The Metamorphosis of Form

A new revolution was at hand in the world of modern dance. In the 1950s a number of choreographers began to question the very nature of dance. Although earlier modern dancers had introduced new dance techniques and subject matter, for the most part they had retained the formalistic values first established by ballet. Choreography was believed to have well-defined principles, which provided the measure of a choreographer's craftsmanship. Music and design ideally supported the choreographer's purposes, and artistic collaboration was the craftsmanlike process of knitting all the elements of a work into a seamless whole. The idea of craftsmanship was also implicit in the belief that dancers should be highly skilled in special dance techniques. The total stage picture was often likened to a moving painting framed by the proscenium. The choreographer played the role of the painter, selecting what the viewer saw and directing his focus to different performers or areas of the stage.

These expectations were exploded in the works of Merce Cunningham, Alwin Nikolais, Paul Taylor and the choreographers who followed them in the 1960s and 70s. A crucial step in the development of their new concept of dance was the abandonment of the idea that dance must tell a story or express emotion. Although this in itself was scarcely a radical notion (ballet choreographers such as Balanchine had discarded narratives while retaining traditional formal structures), these choreographers used the abandonment of narrative as the springboard for daring experiments with form.

Cunningham (b.1919), a former Graham dancer (he had created the role of the revivalist in *Appalachian Spring*), began to choreograph in the early 1940s. From the beginning he frequently collaborated with the avant-garde composer John Cage, who helped shape his ideas. Choreography, music and design are treated as independent entities in Cunningham's works: although music occupies the same timespan as the choreography, and design the same physical space, neither has to relate in any other way to the dancing.

Cunningham liberated choreography from traditional principles of good composition, such as the idea that every dance has a well-defined beginning, middle and end. His belief that 'anything can follow anything' applies both to large structural units, such as the sections of a dance, and smaller ones such as movement phrases (analogous to sentences in grammar). Unlike more

155

106 Yvonne Rainer in Trio A *(1966), which she choreographed. It is one of the most influential works in the modern dance repertoire.*

traditionally structured forms of ballet and modern dance, his choreography is not governed by the logical progression of movements building towards a climax. Nor does he present any one section of the work as more important than another: he has no equivalent of the highly anticipated 'Black Swan Pas de Deux' in *Swan Lake*. He also explored the use of stillness as a deliberate choice, not merely the absence of movement.

The use of stage space also changed in Cunningham's choreography. The 'front and centre' spot traditionally coveted by soloists no longer exists in his works. Dance can take place on any part of the stage; it need not even be frontally orientated, but can be viewed from any angle (at performances in Cunningham's own studio, for instance, audiences are seated in an L-shaped configuration). The viewer's focus is never directed to a particular spot; he must often decide among many centres of activity.

Cunningham's interest in the choreographic process led him to explore ideas of indeterminacy and chance. Indeterminacy means that certain elements in the work are allowed to change from performance to performance. In *Sixteen Dances for Soloist and Company of Three* (1951), the first of his dances to use indeterminacy, the variable was the order of the sections. *Field Dances* (1963) gave each dancer a relatively simple series of movements, which he or she could execute in any order and any number of times, entering and exiting at will. Music, sets and costumes may also be indeterminate: in *Story* (1963), the dancers selected what they would wear at each performance from a pile of secondhand clothing collected by the designer, Robert Rauschenberg, who used materials found in the theatre to assemble a new set at every performance.

Cunningham uses chance procedures to select the components of both indeterminate and fixed dances. In choreographing *Suite by Chance* (1953), the first of his dances to be entirely created through chance procedures, he made charts of elements such as space, time and positions, then tossed a coin to link together movement sequences. *Canfield* (1969) was created by assigning different aspects of movements to different playing cards. Indeterminacy and chance should not be confused with improvisation, for the choreography itself is worked out and rehearsed beforehand. In *Suite by Chance*, for instance, the movement sequences had to be carefully devised so that they could be performed in many different combinations.

The results of this approach to choreography are of course random and arbitrary: Paul Taylor, a former company member, recalls that he learned all the sections of *Dime A Dance* (1953) but never got to dance in it for a whole week of performances, because his number never came up. Cunningham, however, sees randomness and arbitrariness as positive qualities because they are conditions of real life. He values immediacy – the present moment rather

107 Merce Cunningham (foreground) performed with his company in Septet *(1953), a work that is today considered somewhat uncharacteristic of him since its choreography is closely allied to its score by Satie.*

than either the past or the future – and is more interested in process than product. He relishes the challenges of the work in hand, with all its risks and unpredictability.

Cunningham's Events were invented in 1964 to enable his company to perform in many different spaces. They consist of recombinations of complete dances, excerpts from dances and new material, presented without intermission. The first Events took place in museums and gymnasiums; others have been given outdoors (for example, in the Piazza San Marco in Venice) or in his own studio in Manhattan. The viewer is not required to identify the dances, which are not specified on the programme; he is simply invited to enjoy the dancing.

Cunningham is not primarily interested in communicating a story to the audience, though a germ of narrative may spur his creativity. However, his works are not entirely devoid of emotional resonances, and some of them call up powerful associations in the viewer. An often-cited example is *Winterbranch* (1964), which has evoked images of nuclear war, concentration camps and shipwrecks. Cunningham asked Rauschenberg to design lighting

that would give the effect of automobile headlights on a road at night or flashlights that distort shapes in the dark. The atmosphere is bleak, oppressive and desolate; the dancers move with slow deliberation and remain close to the floor, often dragging each other from place to place. Cunningham, however, seldom explains his intentions in any specific work, but leaves the viewer free to interpret it as he will.

Cunningham has long been associated with the artistic and musical avant-garde. Cage, who has been his most frequent musical collaborator, helped him develop his applications of chance and indeterminacy. Cunningham has also worked with the composers Earle Brown, Morton Feldman, Toshi Ichiyanagi, Gordon Mumma, David Tudor, Christian Wolff and others. The artists Jasper Johns, Robert Rauschenberg and Mark Lancaster have designed many works for him; Andy Warhol, Frank Stella and Morris Graves have also contributed designs. Working in collaboration with the filmmaker Charles Atlas, Cunningham became one of the first choreographers to explore the creative potentials of dance on videotape; his first original work for video was *Westbeth* (1974). Cunningham has been recognized during his lifetime as one of the most innovative and influential choreographers of the 20th century.

Unlike Cunningham, Alwin Nikolais (b.1912) generally serves as his own designer and composer, and his multi-media spectacles truly integrate dance,

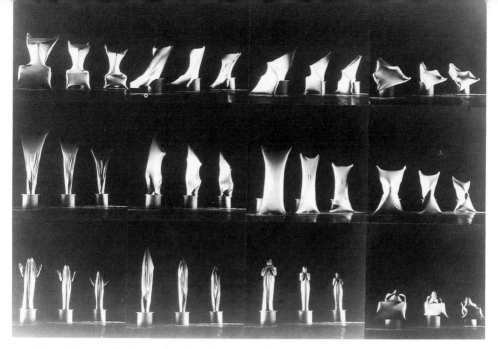

109 Encased in stretchy bags, the three dancers in the 'Noumenon' section of Alwin Nikolais's Masks, Props, and Mobiles *(1953) assume a protean array of shapes.*

music and design. His approach to dance was shaped in part by his early experiences as an accompanist, puppeteer and stage technician. Although he studied dance at Bennington and worked for a time as Hanya Holm's assistant, he rebelled against what he viewed as the modern dance's preoccupation with self. His own world view is cosmic in scope.

He began to put his ideas into practice in the early 1950s when he taught improvisation classes at New York's Henry Street Playhouse, which he also directed. One of his earliest experiments was *Masks, Props, and Mobiles* (1953), which some critics refused to recognize as dance because it used costumes that concealed or transformed the dancers' bodies: in the section titled 'Noumenon', for instance, the dancers were completely encased in bags that were stretched into different shapes by their movements. Nikolais, however, believed that such costumes, masks and props helped the dancers transcend the purely personal or even the human. 'I wanted man to be able to identify with things other than himself', he has stated. 'We must give up our navel contemplations long enough to take our place in space.'

He is often accused of dehumanization because the human presence does not dominate his theatrical world. As in Schlemmer's *Triadic Ballet*, the

159

108 Merce Cunningham's Channels/Inserts *(1981) allows many different points of interest to develop simultaneously on stage.*

dancers' bodies are often altered or concealed by costumes, make-up, props or lighting. Nikolais has been highly successful in his goal of transporting viewers to a world beyond that of human concerns. His dancers are most often likened to extraterrestrial creatures, though they also have called to mind organisms under a microscope or creatures from the bottom of a pond. They seem far removed from our own sphere, farther than the quasi-human sylphs and fairies of the Romantic ballet, for Nikolais's vision has been shaped by science as well as fantasy. He has also compared his work with non-objective art, which does not aim to represent 'real' objects, but instead draws the viewer's attention to its substance – shape, colour, texture, space, time – which becomes the focal point of the work.

In 1953 he retired from performing in order to devote his energies to choreography. He also experimented with tape-recorded sound and electronic music, dyed his own slides (much as Loie Fuller had earlier in the century) and designed costumes, props, scenery and lighting. He used props to extend the human body in *Kaleidoscope* (1955), which has sections titled Discs, Pole, Paddles, Hoop, Straps, Cape and so on. *Prism* (1956) marked the first time that he consciously used light to change the appearance of figures in motion, and his first use of an electronic score. He also experimented with structure: *Kaleidoscope* presented a series of seemingly unrelated events one after another; while *Prism* overlaid one scene upon another, creating a rich texture of sound and motion, a word that Nikolais prefers to 'movement' since it suggests an on-going process rather than a completed action.

Although Fokine might have accused him of neglecting the element of drama, Nikolais believes that 'abstraction does not eliminate emotion'. His works conjure up rituals from a primeval time when humankind still felt awed by the potency of nature's forces. He does not ask his dancers to play roles or emote; his famous exhortation to them is 'Motion, not emotion.' Yet their motion helps build images that are fraught with emotional connotations. Critics have noted that his works frequently end with images of cataclysm. In *Tower* (1965), the dancers construct a tower out of lengths of aluminium, happily decorating it with banners, but an explosion sends it tottering. A real tent plays a central role in *Tent* (1968): it is ceremonially erected by the dancers and serves them as costume and scenery, but it ultimately swallows them. Nikolais's works make their point through the accumulation of images; their whole is greater than the sum of their parts. Like Cunningham's works, they suggest rather than state meanings; the choreographer does not attempt to enforce a message, but allows the viewer a great deal of latitude in interpreting the work.

Movement, which Cunningham and Nikolais saw as a basic component of dance, was emphatically denied in one of Paul Taylor's (b.1930) earliest and most radical works, *Duet* (1957), in which he and his pianist remained motionless for the duration of the dance, which was accompanied by a 'non-score' by John Cage. Also presented on the same programme, titled 'Seven New Dances', was *Epic*, in which Taylor, dressed in a business suit, moved slowly across the stage to the sound of a recorded time announcement. Louis Horst's review of this programme, published in *Dance Observer* of November 1957, consisted of a blank space.

Taylor later said that he wanted to 'go back to basics' in his early dances, using everyday movements such as walking, running and sitting – an objective reminiscent of Isadora Duncan's. However, unlike Duncan, who aimed to transform natural movements into the stuff of art, Taylor sometimes planted the movement equivalents of found objects (*objets trouvés*) in his dances. In *Lost, Found and Lost* (1982), which is based on material from the 'Seven New Dances' programme, a queue of dancers moves one by one into the wings in the manner of people waiting to use a public telephone. The dancers in *Esplanade* (1975) walk, run, jump, slide and fall to the accompaniment of two of Bach's double violin concertos.

Paradoxically, Taylor's most radical experiments were made while he was still active as a dancer in Graham's company, creating roles such as the villainous Aegisthus in *Clytemnestra*. His widely varied experience included a period in Cunningham's company, as well as work with Humphrey, Weidman, Limón, Sokolow and Robbins. The range of his works is as diverse as his background: currents of whimsical humour alternate or even co-exist with explorations into the dark side of human nature, sometimes

110 Paul Taylor (left) created a joyous world filled with love and light in Aureole *(1962).*

111 *The deeply felt religious beliefs expressed in Negro spirituals are given theatrical form in Alvin Ailey's* Revelations *(1960). In this section, images of baptism and spiritual cleansing are enhanced by long white streamers symbolizing water.*

112 *Agile, athletic men and fleet-footed women cavort with lyricism and a touch of humour in Paul Taylor's* Arden Court *(1981).*

with a glimpse of the apocalypse. By far his most popular works are his plotless pieces, which display a delight in lyrical movement. The first of these, *Aureole* (1962), danced to the music of Handel, is now performed by many ballet companies; others of this genre are *Airs* (1978) and *Arden Court* (1981). These sunny-natured dances have made modern dance accessible to a wide segment of the public.

Another popular work, *Three Epitaphs* (1956), depicts the wryly amusing antics of a group of faceless, grotesque but strangely appealing anthropoids, costumed by Rauschenberg in head-to-toe unitards of charcoal grey, decorated with bits of mirror. Equally equivocal are the elegantly dressed ladies and gentlemen of *Cloven Kingdom* (1976), whose animal nature surfaces to the beat of jungle drums. The weird, oversized insect of *Insects and Heroes* (1961) proves to be more wistful than threatening. Taylor frequently plays upon the discrepancies between appearance and reality, deftly upsetting our expectations. Perhaps his strongest demonstration of the unreliability of vision is *Private Domain* (1969), in which the rectangular panels of Alex Katz's set obscure portions of the stage, with the result that each spectator's view of the dance will vary depending upon his seat in the auditorium. Many critics have noted the voyeuristic quality of watching this dance, the psychological interplay between that which is hidden and that which can be seen.

In 1980 Taylor created his own version of a legendary ballet, *The Rite of Spring*, which he subtitled *The Rehearsal*. Danced to a two-piano reduction of Stravinsky's score, this work comprises several layers of meaning: a detective story involving gangsters and a kidnapped baby, a dance rehearsal and an evocation of Nijinsky's ballet (the dance of the bereaved mother parallels that of the Chosen Maiden, while the stamping and heavy jumps of the dancers in the rehearsal recall the tribe's dances). Taylor succeeded in creating a work that was at once original and a homage to the past; unlike many other reworkings of Stravinsky's score, it seems fresh and vibrant.

The experiments of Cunningham, Nikolais and Taylor were extended and often carried to their logical extreme by a number of young choreographers active in the 1960s and 70s, among them Trisha Brown, Lucinda Childs (b.1940), Laura Dean (b.1945), Douglas Dunn (b.1942), Simone Forti (b.1935), David Gordon, Kenneth King, Meredith Monk (b.1943), Steve Paxton (b.1939), Yvonne Rainer (b.1934), Twyla Tharp (b.1942) and others. Many had been students of Cunningham, and several had participated in the freewheeling dance composition classes of Robert Dunn, given at Cunningham's studio. In 1962 Dunn organized the first dance concert at Judson Memorial Church, which became a centre for artistic and intellectual activities and the home of the group known as Judson Dance Theater. This was a period of much cross-fertilization among the arts. The Judson Dance

Theater's performers and choreographers included a number of artists, composers, writers and filmmakers who were not trained dancers; especially notable were the artists Rauschenberg and Robert Morris, and the composer John Herbert McDowell. In addition, many dancers took part in Happenings and other mixed-media or performance art events.

Although these choreographers are often grouped under the rubric of 'post-modern' dancers, their ideas and goals were actually quite diverse. What most of them had in common was an earnest desire to reduce dance to its essentials: hence their emphasis on formal qualities, unobscured by role-playing or purely decorative theatrical trappings such as fanciful costumes and scenery. They rejected too the aura of glamour that the public had come to associate with dancing and dancers. These choreographers had no use for the prettiness of ballet or the soul-searching of earlier modern dancers. Their austere vision necessarily required them to repudiate many of the qualities that had formerly seemed inextricably linked with theatrical dance. As Yvonne Rainer declared in a famous manifesto:

NO to spectacle no to virtuosity no to transformations and magic and make-believe no to the glamour and transcendency of the star image no to the heroic no to the anti-heroic no to trash imagery no to involvement of performer or spectator no to style no to camp no to seduction of spectator by the wiles of the performer no to eccentricity no to moving or being moved.

Out of the work of Rainer and her colleagues there evolved a new definition of theatrical dance, reduced to a minimum: a person (or persons) moving in a space designated as a performing area. The dancer did not, of course, have to be moving at all; as Cunningham and Taylor had earlier shown, stillness was a valid choreographic choice. As in Cunningham's Events, the performing space did not have to be a proscenium stage; it could be anywhere at all. Instead of tutus or even the 'long woolens' of Graham's austere period, these dancers dressed in unassuming practice clothes such as sweatsuits (long before these garments became chic) or in street clothes. Sneakers, not pointe shoes, were the preferred type of footgear.

Although the work of these choreographers is extremely complex and continues to undergo change and development, a few general statements can be made. Many choreographers rejected the notion that dance requires the mastery of a special technique. Instead of technique, everyday movements became the raw material of some dances: in Steve Paxton's *Satisfyin Lover* (1967) performers simply walk across the floor, following given cues. Other pieces featured the wholesale incorporation of ordinary actions: for example, Kenneth King sat at a table reading, then watered a pot of flowers in *Time*

Overleaf *113 An all-male cast engages in a lighthearted athletic competition in Robert North's* Troy Game *(1974), performed here by the Dance Theatre of Harlem.*

Capsule (1974). Such movements acquired interest and value through their context.

In the liberal atmosphere of the Judson Dance Theater, the lack of dance technique was no deterrent to performing or even choreographing. Some choreographers deliberately enlisted untrained performers for their pieces, preferring naturalness or freshness of approach to the more predictable responses of highly trained dancers. Rauschenberg created and danced in *Pelican* (1963), a trio for two men on roller skates and a woman in pointe shoes. Deborah Hay (b.1941) gradually simplified the movements in her dances so that anyone could perform them. Combining elements of meditation and folk dance, her pieces evolved to the point where the audience was superfluous and the dancers performed mainly for their own benefit and enjoyment.

Yet, as Rainer's seminal *Trio A* (1966) proved, movement could be stripped of much of its ornamentation without ceasing to be interesting or challenging in itself. First presented as three simultaneous solos under the title *The Mind Is a Muscle, Part I, Trio A* is performed in a continuous flow of equally stressed movements. There is no climax, and the performer does not attempt to conceal his effort: for example, instead of striking a triumphant arabesque as a ballerina might in *The Sleeping Beauty*, the performer of *Trio A* deliberately allows the audience to perceive the difficulty of balancing on one leg. The performer never looks directly at the audience, never points his toes, never adopts the pulled-up, highly energized stance of most ballet and modern dancers. *Trio A* has been executed by performers of many body types, including non-dancers as well as dancers; it does not require a certain idealized physique to make its effects, as ballet often does. Yet despite its relaxed appearance, *Trio A* demands intelligence and exertion from its performers.

In Twyla Tharp's choreography, the unstressed physical stance of *Trio A* is transformed into a nonchalant carriage of the torso that often contrasts radically with the violent exertions of the arms and legs. Tharp's technique, an eclectic blend of ballet, modern, tap, jazz, social dancing and athletics, represents a new type of virtuosity that parallels ballet's big leaps and multiple pirouettes. Steve Paxton's technique of contact improvisation, in which the performers alternately take each other's weight without using their hands, requires a highly developed sense of balance and a capacity for rapport with others. Similarly, Trisha Brown's *Falling Duet* (1968) demands alertness, ingenuity and good reflexes as the two performers take turns falling and catching one another.

Freed by Cunningham and Nikolais from the necessity of storytelling or self-expression, the choreographers of the sixties began to explore new

106

114, 115 Top, dancing with members of her company in Sue's Leg *(1975), Twyla Tharp (right) draws upon a blend of dance techniques, among them ballet, modern dance and jazz. Below, spinning became a trademark of Laura Dean's work; this is* Song *(1976).*

approaches to conceiving and structuring dances. Like Cunningham, most of these choreographers have been interested in process rather than product. An important influence was the west coast choreographer Anna Halprin (b.1920), who based her dances on games, tasks and improvisation. Simone Forti, who brought Halprin's ideas east, created works in which rules comparable to those of a task or game gave structure to the movement but allowed individual solutions to problems. In *Huddle* (1961), six or seven people formed a dome-shaped cluster with their arms around each other's waists and shoulders. At random, each member of the group disengaged himself from the cluster, which closed up after him, and climbed over it.

Several choreographers have experimented with repetition as a compositional device. Brown's system of accumulations, introduced with a solo in 1971, built the dance as though adding links to a chain. Each movement became a new link and the whole sequence was repeated from the beginning each time a movement was added. In later variations, the performer rotated gradually, eventually making a 360-degree turn; or the movements were performed by a group, sometimes in different positions (for example, propped against a wall); or the dance was 'de-accumulated' by eliminating movements from the beginning of the phrase with each repetition, somewhat in the fashion of a choreographic chain letter. Lucinda Childs's dances move through repeated phrases modulated by subtle and sometimes elusive changes, tracing geometric floor-patterns of astonishing intricacy and complexity. Many viewers have discerned in Laura Dean's works an affinity

115   with folk festivals and rituals; her use of spinning, in particular, is often compared with that of the whirling dervishes of the Middle East. The prolonged repetition in her dances makes the slightest change acquire an inordinate significance.

Meredith Monk, like Nikolais, is a multi-talented artist who composes her own music and writes her own scripts as well as choreographing movement. She was nominally a member of the Judson group and shared their desire for experimentation and their use of unconventional movement, unconventional structures and mixed-media. However, she differed from them in her interest in symbolism and spectacle, and her works demonstrated a dramatic intent that was at variance with the prevailing emphasis on formalism. Yet Monk's pieces do not follow the type of linear narrative utilized in traditional works such as *Swan Lake*. Carrying further Graham's practice of breaking up the chronological flow of events with flashbacks, she presents images and events in a disjointed, non-consecutive fashion that may initially seem random or fortuitous. As the viewer watches, meanings gradually emerge.

Vessel (1971) was inspired by the story of Joan of Arc. It took place in three different locations in the course of an evening. The audience assembled at

116 Ashton's Rhapsody *(1980) is a show-case for the breathtaking virtuosity of the Russian dancer Mikhail Baryshnikov.*

Monk's loft, where the black-clad performers took turns appearing as the characters they would play: a king, a madwoman, a wizard and so forth. In the second section of the work, which was set at The Performing Garage, the characters performed various actions – putting herbs into a kettle, reading, mixing chemicals – within the frame of a 'handmade mountain' of white muslin, which gave them the appearance of figures in a tapestry. Joan (played by Monk) underwent her trial here, questioned by a pair of bishops. The piece concluded in a vast and shadowy parking lot, where Joan ultimately danced into the distance and vanished into a welder's shower of sparks.

A few choreographers made political statements in dance during the period of protest in the late 1960s and early 1970s. While recuperating from an operation, Rainer danced *Trio A*, renamed *Convalescent Dance* for the occasion, on a programme protesting against the Vietnam War in 1967. Working with a group of Vietnam veterans who opposed the war, Paxton created *Collaboration with Wintersoldier* (1971), in which two upside-down performers watched the group's film about Vietnam. As in the 1930s, dancers voiced their beliefs through their art.

Like Cunningham, many choreographers found unconventional locations for their dances. Some of Monk's works, such as *Vessel*, have required the audience to travel from one place to another. The first section of her three-part *Juice* (1969) occupied all the spiralling levels of the Guggenheim Museum. The piece then diminished in scale: its second section was presented in a proscenium theatre and the third in Monk's loft. Performed at dusk in New York's Central Park, Tharp's *Medley* (1969) was something of an exercise in perception for the viewers as they watched the widely scattered figures of the dancers in the waning light. Brown's *Roof Piece* (1971), spread out over twelve blocks in lower Manhattan, recalled the party game 'Gossip'. Stationed on rooftops, the dancers relayed movements from one to another, trying to reproduce them with the least amount of distortion. In all of these works, the unusual locations were not used simply for the sake of novelty; they had real effects upon the choreography and the audience's perceptions.

Several choreographers of the 1960s and 70s followed Nikolais's example in using modern technology in their works. Monk first employed film in *16 Millimeter Earrings* (1966), at one point projecting inflated images of her face upon a white drum concealing her head. She has since included film and slide projections in many of her productions. From 1968 to 1972 Brown experimented with 'equipment pieces' that enabled her to exploit hitherto neglected performing areas such as walls and ceilings. Supported by ropes, pulleys, mountain-climbing gear and the like, the dancers in *Walking on the Wall* (1971) and other works strove to maintain a normal upright walking position. Many viewers reported feeling spatially disorientated while

*117 Trisha Brown
utilized hitherto neglected
spaces in 'equipment
pieces' such as* Man
Walking Down the
Side of a Building
(1970).

watching these pieces, as though they were looking down from tall buildings onto the sidewalks below.

Although the more extreme experiments of the 1950s, 60s and 70s were abandoned or softened with the passage of the years, their impact has inescapably changed our conceptions of dance. There is now more latitude in the types of movement generally accepted as dance, and more freedom of choice in choreographic method, performing style, costume, performing space and other elements of presentation. Although the Judson Dance Theater's use of untrained performers did not become pervasive, it helped dissolve the myth that a dancer had to be trained practically from the cradle. The inherent experimentalism of modern dance in its many forms held great appeal in an era devoted to self-discovery and self-expression. As the narrow definition of dance widened, more people began to approach dance as something to do as well as to watch. The number of dance students, performers, choreographers and productions began to rise. Dance was on its way to becoming a mainstream art.

CHAPTER ELEVEN

A Time of Growth

Ballet slowly but surely expanded into a global activity in the decades following the mid-century. There are now more ballet companies than ever before, even in countries that do not share the European heritage, such as Turkey, Iran, Japan and China. The possession of a ballet company has become a sign of cultural achievement and a source of civic or national pride. This is borne out by the fact that many companies are called after their places of origin: London Festival Ballet, Scottish Ballet, Netherlands Dance Theatre, National Ballet of Canada, Ballet Nacional de Cuba, Australian Ballet, Central Ballet of China and others. Two older companies have assumed new names indicative of their status as cultural representatives of their countries: the Sadler's Wells Ballet became Britain's Royal Ballet upon receiving its royal charter in 1956, while Ballet Theatre took the name American Ballet Theatre in 1957.

Companies that previously enjoyed a primarily local appeal increasingly perform abroad, building international reputations for themselves. The Royal Danish Ballet, active since the 18th century, began to tour in the 1950s, sharing its unrivalled trove of lovingly preserved ballets by the great 19th-century choreographer Bournonville. The Bolshoi Ballet first appeared in the west in the 1950s, followed by the Kirov in 1961. In exchange, American Ballet Theatre and the New York City Ballet have both danced in the U.S.S.R. 32

With the spread of ballet to different parts of the world, company repertories have become more varied. In addition to old favourites such as *Giselle*, *Coppélia*, *The Nutcracker* and *Les Sylphides*, many companies present new works by contemporary choreographers and pieces with a national or ethnic flavour. London Festival Ballet and the National Ballet of Canada were initially known for their productions of the classics, which are useful to fledgling companies since they provide valuable training for young dancers and challenging parts for established stars. London Festival Ballet's prima ballerina, Markova, was a noted interpreter of the role of Giselle, as was Alicia Alonso (b.1921), who danced the role for many years at the head of the company she founded, the Ballet Nacional de Cuba. Both companies now perform a mixture of classic and contemporary ballets.

In contrast, some companies began with the aim of spotlighting the talents of locally born choreographers. Les Grands Ballets Canadiens, founded in

118 Anthony Dowell, as the tutor Beliaev, and Lynn Seymour, as Natalia Petrovna, in a tender moment in Ashton's ballet version of Turgenev's play A Month in the Country, *first performed by the Royal Ballet in 1976.*

Montreal by Ludmilla Chiriaeff (a former member of de Basil's Ballets Russes), commissions many of its ballets from the Canadians Brian Macdonald, Fernand Nault and James Kudelka. Some of these works have reflected the company's French Canadian origins, such as Macdonald's *Tam Ti Delam* (1974), a lighthearted tribute to life in Quebec.

The traditional movement of choreographers from one company to another has often served to enrich repertories. During her affiliation with American Ballet Theatre in the 1950s, Birgit Cullberg (b.1908) restaged her masterly dance-drama *Miss Julie*, which she had first produced in her native Sweden in 1950. Based on August Strindberg's play, *Miss Julie* tells the story of a discontented aristocrat who seduces her butler, then kills herself in shame at her betrayal of her rank. The role of the opportunistic butler, who responds with lust to Julie's advances yet treacherously assists in her suicide, revealed the dramatic gifts of Erik Bruhn (1928–86), a Danish dancer who had previously been known mainly for his nobility and elegance in princely roles.

As in the past, some companies are dominated by a single choreographer, who occasionally gives the company his name. The ballets of Gerald Arpino (b.1928) have been a constant element in the repertory of Robert Joffrey's ensemble, now called the Joffrey Ballet, since its founding in 1956. The Brussels-based Ballet du XXe Siècle (Ballet of the Twentieth Century), founded in 1960, performs principally the works of Maurice Béjart (b.1927). Eliot Feld (b.1942), who began as a dancer and choreographer with American Ballet Theatre, now directs the second of the two companies founded by him, the Feld Ballet, which gave its first performance in 1974.

Ballets: U.S.A. was organized by Jerome Robbins in 1958 as a showcase for his works. *New York Export: Opus Jazz* (1958) graphically depicts the 'cool' mentality cultivated by urban youth of the time: a budding romance quickly lapses into indifference; in another episode five boys gang-rape a girl, then casually toss her off a rooftop. Robbins also restaged ballets he had originally created for the New York City Ballet. *The Cage* (1951) is a horrific vision of a tribe of castrating insect-women, while *Afternoon of a Faun* (1953), danced to the same Debussy tone poem that inspired Nijinsky, portrays a fleeting encounter between two young dancers in a studio. In contrast, *The Concert* (1956) hilariously pictures the fantasies of concertgoers listening to piano pieces by Chopin. After this company dissolved in 1961, Robbins worked for a time in the musical theatre, then returned to the New York City Ballet, which he now heads together with the Danish dancer and choreographer Peter Martins (b.1946).

During the 1950s and 60s, many companies searched for new approaches to ballet in order to broaden its appeal. At this time a large segment of the public perceived ballet as an elitist entertainment, or dismissed it as a

119, 120 Left, *primarily admired for his princely grace, Erik Bruhn proved that he was also capable of dramatic roles such as the treacherous butler in Birgit Cullberg's* Miss Julie *(first performed in 1950). Cynthia Gregory danced the title role in this performance by American Ballet Theatre. Right, an outsize puppet of Diaghilev looms over Nijinsky (Jorge Donn), who jumps through a hoop held by a dancer-Diaghilev (Pierre Dobrievich) in Maurice Béjart's* Nijinsky – Clown of God *(1971).*

tradition-bound holdover from the past. Both of these preconceptions were gradually changed. The physicality of ballet and dance in general attracted the Woodstock generation, which also valued body-orientated disciplines such as nonverbal communication. Ballet themes, so often considered old-fashioned or out of touch with reality, were renovated in the search for relevance that swept the U.S. in the late 1960s.

The modern dance was a key influence in updating ballet's image. Although the modern dancers of the 1930s and 40s had been the resolute foes of ballet, which they derided for its artificiality and escapism, the antagonism between the two camps had softened over the years. Dancers such as Glen Tetley (b.1926) and Robert Joffrey (b.1930) trained in both ballet and modern dance techniques. In their choreography they began to evolve a hybrid form, sometimes called modern ballet. Virtuosic ballet steps such as multiple pirouettes, big leaps and high arabesques coexist with the falls, floorwork and supple torso movements found in modern dance. Pointe work is optional; the dancers sometimes perform in bare feet. This hybrid form tends to emphasize strength, forcefulness and large-scale effects. Its impact is immediate, and the viewer need not be familiar with the fine points of dance technique in order to appreciate it. The sheer physical excitement it generates has made it a favourite with present-day audiences.

As a result of the development of the hybrid form, the distinction between ballet and modern dance, which had been clear-cut in the 1930s and 40s, became more problematic. Many choreographers and their works can no longer be neatly pigeonholed as either ballet or modern dance, and even when the two can be distinguished, each may prove to have absorbed characteristics of the other: the freer use of the torso in ballet, for instance; or a stretched-out line and pointed feet in modern dance.

In addition to assimilating certain aspects of modern dance technique, ballet choreographers began to treat the type of 'ugly' themes that were previously considered the province of modern dance. Tetley's *Pierrot Lunaire* (1962) uses the commedia dell'arte characters Pierrot, Columbine, and Brighella to tell the story of a dreamer's initiation into the harsh realities of life. In *Monument for a Dead Boy* (1965), which Rudi Van Dantzig created for the Dutch National Ballet, a homosexual at the point of death relives his tormented past.

In a more positive vein, the energy and virtuosity of the hybrid form has made it ideally suited to ballets that celebrate the dancers' youth, strength and vitality. Many of Arpino's works for the Joffrey Ballet fit this description. *Trinity* (1969), which is danced to a rock music score, presents the dancers as glorious athletes who execute dazzling leaps and turns with an air of exuberant abandon. The ballet closes with a candlelit ritual reminiscent of the protest marches of the 1960s. Arpino has continued to work in this style, highlighting the prowess of the Joffrey's fine dancers.

Béjart's ballet spectacles of the 1960s, often performed before mass audiences in large performance spaces such as sports arenas and circuses, advocated many of the counterculture's ideals, particularly the 'make love, not war' philosophy of the hippies. These works were often intended to be provocatively iconoclastic, but many critics felt that Béjart's ideas lacked definition and clarity, although his dancers performed with conviction. In his ballet danced to Beethoven's Ninth Symphony (1964), which was preceded by excerpts from the writings of the German philosopher Friedrich Nietzsche, Béjart tried to express his ideas on love, liberty and the ideal world. *Firebird* (1970) was conceived as a political fable in which a red-clad male Firebird leads a group of rebels to victory. Béjart's attraction to Asian

121 Productions of the classics today form an important focus for American Ballet Theatre. Mikhail Baryshnikov, who has danced regularly with the company, is seen here partnering Cynthia Harvey in his revival of Marius Petipa's Don Quixote in 1978.

religion and mysticism – he named his ballet school Mudra, after the Hindu word for hand gestures – inspired *Bhakti* (1968), which depicts three pairs of famous lovers from Hindu mythology.

Although the political overtones of Béjart's works have generally diminished with the passage of the years, he continues to favour flamboyant theatrical effects, often combining many media, and he is known as a consummate showman. In *Nijinsky – Clown of God* (1971) he evokes the *120* famous dancer's legend through images drawn from Nijinsky's best-known roles and quotations from his diary. Diaghilev is represented by a huge puppet, and the inspirational figure of Nijinsky's wife by a woman in a pink Edwardian gown. Béjart himself played the role of Mephistopheles in *Notre Faust* (1975), presenting Goethe's tempter as a master of ceremonies, complete with microphone.

A similar passion for mixed-media theatre touched American ballet as well as modern dance in the 1960s. Joffrey's *Astarte* (1967), which gained notoriety as the first psychedelic ballet, combined the action on stage with film, strobe lighting and an acid-rock score. This pas de deux depicted a man (a male dancer) who rises from a seat in the audience and mounts to the stage for a hallucinatory erotic encounter with a tattooed love goddess.

Many choreographers of the 1970s and 80s continue to use the hybrid form. Jiří Kylián (b.1947), who became the artistic director of the Netherlands Dance Theatre in 1975, seldom works with a plot or specific characters, but he nevertheless creates strong images of universal human emotions such as exultation and grief. His ballets, which are closely linked to their music, are noted for their speed, virtuosity and sweeping sense of movement. *Soldiers' Mass* (1980) was inspired by the true story of a group of raw young Czech recruits who met their deaths in the First World War. Its twelve-man cast often moves in unison as if to express shared fears and tensions. Reflecting moods of religious affirmation and doubt, the dancers are exuberant and subdued by turns in Stravinsky's *Symphony of Psalms* (1978).

Like Kylián, the Singapore-born choreographer Choo San Goh (b.1948) is not primarily concerned with storytelling, though he has mounted a version of *Romeo and Juliet* (Boston Ballet, 1984). He is best known for his plotless ballets, staged for a number of companies. In ballets such as *Momentum* (1979) and *Helena* (1980), both created for the Joffrey Ballet, his choreography conveys a sense of mood, yet the most striking characteristic of his work is the intricate patterning of groups, achieved through compositional devices such as canon form and counterpoint.

Although Alvin Ailey (b.1931), who danced in Lester Horton's company, is usually classified as a modern dancer, he often employs the hybrid form in works created for his multi-racial group, the Alvin Ailey American Dance Theater. His movement style is further enriched by Afro-American and jazz dancing, and his themes frequently focus on the black heritage. *Revelations* (1960), the company's signature piece, is danced to Negro spirituals. Its high point is the duet 'Fix Me, Jesus', in which a woman's religious yearnings are expressed with the literal and figurative support of a sympathetic man, perhaps a preacher. 'Wading in the Water' depicts a baptism in a river, symbolized by blue and white streamers. The ballet closes with the energetic 'Rocka My Soul in the Bosom of Abraham', a rousing audience-pleaser.

Another ethnically-oriented company is the Dance Theatre of Harlem. It was founded by Arthur Mitchell (b.1934), a former principal dancer of Balanchine's New York City Ballet, with the aim of proving that black dancers could excel in classical ballet as well as in ethnic and modern dance. The company performs a number of Balanchine's masterworks, including *Serenade*, *Agon* and *The Four Temperaments*. Its Creole version of *Giselle*

122 A tattooed love goddess (Trinette Singleton) exerts her power over a mortal man (Maximiliano Zomosa) in Robert Joffrey's 'psychedelic ballet' Astarte *(1967).*

(1984) reconciles the contrasting classical and ethnic currents in black dance by retaining the traditional choreography while transferring the action from medieval Germany to 19th-century Louisiana, where the well-to-do free blacks looked down upon their more recently freed fellows. As in the original ballet, Giselle and her lover are separated by class barriers.

Other minority groups in the U.S. have also formed their own dance companies. Ballet Hispanico, organized in New York City by Tina Ramirez in 1970, dances works by many choreographers, but each piece has some bearing on Spanish or Latin American history or culture. The dancers are trained in flamenco and other forms of Spanish dancing as well as ballet, modern and jazz.

Modern dance choreographers first began to set pieces for ballet companies in the late 1940s, when Bettis created *Virginia Sampler* for the Ballet Russe de Monte Carlo and Cunningham staged *The Seasons* (1947) for Ballet Society. *Episodes* (1959), a much-publicized collaboration between

Balanchine and Graham, was actually two separate, highly individualistic works, both of which have been presented independently. The two pieces had little more in common than their use of Anton Webern's music, for Graham mounted a dance-drama symbolically depicting the power-struggle between Mary Queen of Scots and Elizabeth I of England, while Balanchine staged a plotless ballet danced in leotards and tights. The modern dance choreographer John Butler (b. 1920) created one of the Harkness Ballet's most popular works, *After Eden* (1966), a pas de deux evoking the sufferings of Adam and Eve after their expulsion from paradise.

The practice of commissioning ballets from modern dance choreographers became more frequent in the 1970s. Tharp has been a favourite guest choreographer. The breezy humour of her dances in *Deuce Coupe* (1973), created for members of the Joffrey Ballet and her own company, matches the accompanying pop songs by the Beach Boys. In piquant contrast to the colourfully-dressed dancers moving in Tharp's eclectic style, a white-clad girl diligently works her way through an alphabetical list of academic ballet steps. Tharp has also mounted works for American Ballet Theatre, featuring the Russian premier danseur Mikhail Baryshnikov (b. 1948) as the puckish leader of *Push Comes to Shove* (1976). At the New York City Ballet, she and Robbins collaborated on *Brahms/Handel* (1984). American Ballet Theatre also commissioned Ailey's *The River* (1970), a plotless work to music by Duke Ellington. *Night* (1980) was the first of several pieces created by Laura Dean for the Joffrey Ballet, all incorporating her trademark movement, spinning.

The National Choreography Project (NCP), established in 1984, has encouraged many American dance companies to take new risks by funding their collaboration with progressive choreographers. The companies thus gain new pieces for their repertories, while the choreographers benefit from wider exposure of their creations and the opportunity to work with large-scale groups. The NCP is jointly supported by the Rockefeller Foundation, Exxon Corporation and the National Endowment for the Arts, and is administered by Pentacle, a New York-based service organization. To date most of its awards have brought together modern dance choreographers and ballet companies. David Gordon's *Field, Chair and Mountain* (1985), which the NCP commissioned for American Ballet Theatre, wittily played upon the interactions between the cast and a complement of folding metal chairs.

Some companies have continued to use more conventional means of wooing audiences. Story-telling ballets have never completely gone out of fashion and in fact many people prefer them to plotless works for much the same reason that they like representational art better than abstract art: the narrative or subject matter provides a convenient 'handle' to the piece. The

115

123 *With increasing frequency, ballet companies are inviting modern dance choreographers to revitalize their repertories. David Gordon's* Field, Chair and Mountain *(1985) was commissioned for the American Ballet Theatre with the help of a grant from the National Choreography Project.*

concise one-act form favoured by Fokine is used by some choreographers, while others prefer to mount evening-long works in the tradition of Petipa.

Among the former is Ashton's *The Dream* (Royal Ballet, 1964), an 124 adaptation of Shakespeare's *A Midsummer Night's Dream* that focuses on the quarrel and reconciliation of the fairy rulers Titania and Oberon, roles memorably created by the British dancers Antoinette Sibley (b.1939) and Anthony Dowell (b.1943). Despite the ballet's compactness Ashton contrives to cover the play's highlights, such as the misadventures of the four human lovers in the woods and the bittersweet encounter between Titania and the unrefined Bottom, who has been fitted with a donkey's head by Oberon's mischievous henchman, Puck.

Kenneth MacMillan (b.1929), who succeeded Ashton as chief choreographer of the Royal Ballet, has produced many evening-long dramatic works.

124, 125 *The Royal Ballet has seen several classic partnerships in recent years. When Anthony Dowell and Antoinette Sibley were paired as Oberon and Titania in Ashton's* The Dream *(1964), a seemingly magical chemistry was revealed (left). The partnership of Margot Fonteyn and Rudolf Nureyev (below) added special intensity to the roles of the doomed lovers in Kenneth MacMillan's* Romeo and Juliet *(1965).*

126 *Although several Soviet choreographers have tackled the subject of* Spartacus, *the story of a slave rebellion in ancient Rome, the definitive version was created by Yuri Grigorovich for the Bolshoi Ballet in 1968.*

In his version of *Romeo and Juliet* (1965), the bustling townspeople of Verona and the warring families of the Montagues and Capulets form the backdrop to the love story of the ill-fated teenaged protagonists. *Manon* (1974) follows the career of an eighteenth-century woman of pleasure from her first innocent love to her death in exile in the wilds of Louisiana. A historical incident, the murder-suicide of Crown Prince Rudolf of Austria-Hungary and his mistress Mary Vetsera, inspired *Mayerling* (1978). These ballets were staged in spectacular style, with large casts and many changes of costume and scenery, reminiscent of the heyday of the Imperial Russian Ballet.

Upon assuming the post of chief choreographer of the Bolshoi Ballet in 1964, Yuri Grigorovich (b.1927) introduced a new emphasis on movement, replacing the long, often heavy-handed mime sequences of older Russian ballets with dancing. His four-act version of *Spartacus* (1968) depicts the rebellion led by the slave Spartacus against the Roman legions commanded by Crassus. The many battle scenes provided a pretext for virile dances by an ensemble of soldiers, slaves and gladiators, while tenderness and pathos were expressed by Phrygia, Spartacus's loyal wife.

185

127 The Swedish choreographer Mats Ek, son of Birgit Cullberg, set the second scene of his Giselle *(1982) in a lunatic asylum rather than the traditional haunted forest, with the wilis as patients in white hospital gowns instead of spirits in tutus.*

The Stuttgart Ballet, based in the city where Noverre spent many fruitful years, flowered in the 1960s under the leadership of the South African–born choreographer John Cranko (1927–73). His narrative ballets, which included versions of Shakespeare's *Romeo and Juliet* and *The Taming of the Shrew*, brought international recognition to the company and its principal dancers Marcia Haydée (b.1939), a Brazilian ballerina with a flair for drama, and the American Richard Cragun (b.1944). Haydée was particularly touching as Tatiana in Cranko's *Onegin* (1965), which was based upon Pushkin's verse novel. In the letter scene of this ballet she convincingly portrayed an adolescent girl racked by first love, who feverishly writes to her beloved, then conjures up his image to join her in an ecstatic pas de deux.

128 A stylized and spectacular adaptation of Shakespeare's play, Ballet Rambert's The Tempest *(1979) has been praised for the unified vision of the choreographer Glen Tetley, the designer Nadine Baylis, and the composer Arne Nordheim. In this scene Ariel (Gianfranco Paoluzi) regards the lovers Ferdinand and Miranda (Mark Wraith and Lucy Burge).*

Balanchine occasionally created dramatic ballets, and sometimes assumed the mimed title role of *Don Quixote* (1965), in which his muse, the American ballerina Suzanne Farrell (b. 1945), played the Don's ideal woman, Dulcinea. Although this ballet contained a disappointingly small amount of dancing, it delivered its interrelated themes of idealism, integrity and faith with great conviction. The Don's many adventures (including the famous episode of tilting at the windmill) result in several beatings and his eventual death, but he is repeatedly solaced by Dulcinea, whose many guises include a maidservant who washes his feet and dries them with her hair.

The great ballets of the past have frequently inspired present-day choreographers. Some attempt to revive the originals as faithfully as possible, aiming to recapture the spirit if not the letter of the past. Ashton's delightful recreation of Dauberval's *La Fille mal gardée* (1960) was achieved with the help of the dance historian Ivor Guest, who unearthed the ballet's original score. The French choreographer Pierre Lacotte (b. 1932) reconstructed *La Sylphide* (first stage version, 1972) with the help of Filippo Taglioni's notes. The Joffrey Ballet has produced many revivals of historical ballets, notably Massine's *Le Tricorne* (1969) and *Parade* (1973). A complete version of Petipa's *La Bayadère* was staged for American Ballet Theatre in 1980 by the Russian ballerina Natalia Makarova (b. 1940). Revivals lure audiences with the promise of seeing something that made history. They have also served indirectly as an educational tool, increasing public awareness of ballet's rich heritage.

Although most companies approach revivals with reverence, some choreographers choose to give a new twist to ballets of the past. In doing so they parallel innovative drama and opera productions such as Peter Brook's *A Midsummer Night's Dream* (1970), which transformed Shakespeare's courtiers, artisans and fairies into white-garbed circus performers. New interpretations of the old generally attract attention through novelty or shock but some explore intriguing possibilities or provide fresh insights.

Erik Bruhn's *Swan Lake* (National Ballet of Canada, 1966) recast the evil sorcerer as a female figure and implied that the hero, Siegfried, was the victim of an Oedipus complex. *Illusions – Like Swan Lake*, which the American choreographer John Neumeier (b. 1942) choreographed for the Hamburg Ballet in 1976, took as its hero King Ludwig of Bavaria, known for his insanity and his obsession with swans. In the second act, a segment of Ivanov's choreography is presented as a ballet-within-a-ballet, which so enthralls the king that he takes the place of the dancer playing Siegfried. Ludwig's fiancée, Natalia, appears in a swan costume in the third-act ballroom scene. Like the original protagonists of *Swan Lake*, Ludwig meets his death by drowning.

In a modern version of *Giselle*, created in 1982 by Mats Ek (b. 1945) for

129 *The musical* A Chorus Line *(1975) explored the lives of 'gypsies', or show dancers, with humour and poignancy.*

Sweden's Cullberg Ballet, Giselle's behaviour in the first act suggests that she 127 is the village idiot. The second act is set in a madhouse, where Giselle and her fellow patients in their white hospital gowns take the place of the Wilis. The beleaguered Albrecht finally appears nude, symbolically purified and ready to start a new life.

Ballet made newspaper headlines in 1961 when Rudolf Nureyev (b. 1938), a soloist with the Kirov Ballet, defected from the Soviet Union. His example was subsequently followed by his compatriots Natalia Makarova, Alexander Godunov and Mikhail Baryshnikov. Nureyev's arrival inspired a second spring in the career of the British ballerina Margot Fonteyn, who became his 125 most frequent partner during his tenure at the Royal Ballet. Ashton created *Marguerite and Armand* (1963), a retelling of the younger Alexandre Dumas's story of the Lady of the Camellias, in tribute to the potent sense of romance they generated on stage. Nureyev's career has been, for the most part, peripatetic: he has danced with companies all over the world and even ventured to perform in modern dance pieces such as Graham's *Appalachian Spring*, Taylor's *Aureole*, and Limón's *The Moor's Pavane*. He has also gained some degree of fame as a choreographer, particularly for his versions of

45 *Romeo and Juliet* (London Festival Ballet, 1977) and *The Nutcracker* (Royal Swedish Ballet, 1967).

In addition to heightening public interest in dance in general, Nureyev helped boost the prestige of the male dancer. Gene Kelly and Edward Villella (b.1936), a principal dancer of the New York City Ballet, also fought against the widespread prejudice against male dancing, which had persisted in the U.S. despite the efforts of Shawn and his Men Dancers. Kelly's television programme 'Dancing Is a Man's Game' (1958) equated dancing with sports, while Villella's phenomenal strength and stamina were extolled on the Bell Telephone Hour's telecast 'Man Who Dances' (1968) and a *Life* magazine article by David Martin, titled 'Is This Man the Country's Best Athlete?' (1969). More than anyone else, however, Nureyev proved that virility need not be incompatible with artistic genius. Thanks to the efforts of these men, more boys and men than ever before now study dance.

From the late 1960s on, ballet and modern dance began to enjoy more attention from the media. National magazines such as *Time*, *Newsweek* and *Saturday Review* began to carry dance reviews with increasing frequency, and dance was occasionally spotlighted in *Life* magazine's photographic spreads. Joffrey's psychedelic ballet *Astarte* appeared on the cover of *Time* in 1968. Television programmes such as Camera Three, the Bell Telephone Hour and the Ed Sullivan Show made dance available to many Americans who had never seen a live performance. Public television's *Dance in America* series, founded in 1975, brought viewers high-quality performances of the works of Ailey, Ashton, Balanchine, Cunningham, Graham, Robbins, Taylor, Tharp and many others, presented by major ballet and modern dance companies. Since 1985, avant-garde dance has had its own television series, *Alive from Off-Center*, co-produced by KCTA/Minneapolis-St Paul and the Walker Art Center.

129 The popularity of dance inspired a plethora of musical comedies and films that took dancing or dancers as their subject matter. *A Chorus Line* (1975), which became Broadway's longest running musical in 1983, was conceived, directed and choreographed by Michael Bennett (1943–87) in the form of an audition that exposed the struggles and uncertainties of Broadway dancers. *Dancin'* (1978) was created by Bob Fosse (b.1927) as a showcase for various types of theatrical dancing, among them ballet, tap and soft-shoe. Fosse's semi-autobiographical film *All That Jazz* (1980), the story of a director who undergoes heart surgery, included prolonged dance sequences, some representing the director's hallucinations. The 1983 revival of *On Your Toes*, choreographed by Peter Martins and Donald Saddler, allowed Natalia Makarova to reveal her gifts as a comic actress in the role of the lustful prima ballerina.

130 *In* The Watteau Duets *(1985), Karole Armitage deploys the pointe shoe*
as a weapon rather than an instrument of airy grace.

A melodramatic rivalry between two female dancers and the story of a young ballerina's rising career supplied the dramatic impetus of *The Turning Point* (1977), which elevated the brilliant Baryshnikov to film stardom. Baryshnikov later played a Russian defector, a role akin to his own life, in *White Nights* (1986), a film that contrasted his classical ballet technique with the tap dancing of a black dancer, Gregory Hines. *Nijinsky* (1980), a film biography of the legendary Russian star, included excerpts from historic ballets such as *Schéhérazade*, *Le Spectre de la Rose* and *L'Aprés-midi d'un faune*, performed by the London Festival Ballet. A mixture of jazz, gymnastics and break-dancing dominated *Flashdance* (1983), the tale of a girl who is a welder by day and a 'flashdancer' by night, and aspires to enter a ballet academy.

Grants from both government and private organizations have contributed immeasurably to the growth of dance by providing a much-needed base of support for the activities of choreographers and dancers. In the U.S., a major source of financial aid is the National Endowment for the Arts (NEA), established in 1965. In addition to awarding grants to companies across the nation, it also organized, in 1968, the Dance Touring Program, which has helped introduce dance to new audiences. The NEA has also supported scholarly organizations such as the Dance Notation Bureau and the Dance Collection of the New York Public Library. In 1963 the Ford Foundation made a historic grant of $7,756,000, the largest sum then awarded to dance, to seven companies and their affiliated schools; it has also made numerous other grants to dance. The Guggenheim Foundation has aided individual dancers, choreographers, scholars and critics. Government support for dance has historically been far more generous in countries other than the U.S. Students are often trained in state-subsidized dance academies, and dancers who are accepted by the national companies frequently receive the salaries and benefits of civil servants, including pensions after retirement. Some countries also provide financial aid for dance writers, researchers and scholars as well as performers and choreographers.

Regional and civic ballet companies have sprung up in many American communities. These are usually non-profit groups that function on a non- or semi-professional basis, though some eventually achieve full professional status. They serve as a traning ground and showcase for budding dancers and choreographers, and help develop audiences for dance in cities and towns that are rarely visited by the major companies. In 1956 Dorothy Alexander of the Atlanta Ballet organized the first regional ballet festival in order to give companies an opportunity to perform for their peers. Her idea was taken up by Josephine and Hermene Schwarz of Dayton, Ohio, who have also been instrumental in the development of regional ballet. Today regional festivals take place across the country. Information and assistance is provided by the

National Association for Regional Ballet, which often sponsors conferences and workshops where companies may share ideas and upgrade the quality of their productions.

Folk dance ensembles have also contributed to the rise of interest in dance. Their repertories usually focus on ritual, recreational or social dances, adapted for stage presentation. The most venerable of these groups is the Moiseyev Folk Dance Ensemble, which grew out of a troupe formed by Igor Moiseyev in Moscow in 1937, though it did not appear in the west until the 1950s. It performs works from all parts of the Soviet Union as well as other countries. Other popular folk dance ensembles include Poland's Mazowsze; the Inbal Dance Theatre of Israel, which initially specialized in Yemenite dances; and the Ballet Folklorico de Mexico.

By the 1970s, observers of the cultural scene had noted a 'dance boom'. More dance companies than ever before were performing, and the audience for dance had grown to unprecedented numbers. The public was beginning to realize that it did not have to comprehend the fine points of technique in order to share in the exhilaration of a leap or the thrill of a plunging fall. Ballet and modern dance were growing more democratic in the sense that their audiences encompassed many different levels of society.

Great popularity can have mixed results: some observers fear that artistic standards will be compromised as companies vie to attract audiences. Others believe that increased competition will raise standards, especially as audiences become more sophisticated. The dance boom has already had many beneficial effects on the dance community. Increased public interest has encouraged many companies to give more performances, and more dancers are now employed for greater lengths of time. Young choreographers have more outlets for their work. Funding organizations are more willing to aid dance as well as literature, painting and music. Notators, critics, researchers and historians – the professions that support dance – are finding more opportunities to exercise their skills.

For the most part, however, it is too soon to assess the effects of the dance boom. Many of the choreographers mentioned in this chapter are still active, and some are still evolving their styles. As in all history, some individuals and their ideas may prove to be no more than a nine-days' wonder, rapidly raised to celebrity and as quickly forgotten. Yet, to those of us living in the midst of it, the dance boom has undoubtedly enhanced the vitality, diversity and accessibility of the art of dance.

131 *The pool of water in which Pina Bausch's* Arien *(1979) takes place is inhabited, logically enough, by a hippopotamus.*

CHAPTER TWELVE

Some Recent Trends

Dance today maintains a high level of activity, encouraged by ever-rising public demand. One proof of this is the increased receptivity to modern dance, which past audiences found more difficult to appreciate than ballet because they perceived it as lacking in ballet's decorative appeal. Today, however, modern dance is extraordinarily diverse and often rivals ballet for glamour and fantasy, both on stage and off. Graham's dancers now wear costumes designed by the couturier Halston; Cunningham and other avant-garde choreographers are now fêted by the fashionable world.

In recent years modern dance has gained new ground in countries such as France, Britain and Japan, as well as in its two birthplaces, the U.S. and Germany. In all of these countries there has been a swing away from the formalism that came to dominate American modern dance in the 1960s. Symbolism, narrative and stage effects, forsworn by Rainer in her famous manifesto, are regaining their importance as means of communication. Though some American choreographers have consistently used these elements (Graham and Monk spring immediately to mind), they seemed to be outnumbered by those who followed the example of Cunningham and the Judson group. Today, however, choreographers are once more rediscovering the values of expression and theatricality, though the strongest shift in favour of these qualities has occurred outside the U.S.

The new narrative style of modern dance generally defies conventional story-telling techniques. The events in these dances seldom proceed in linear or chronological order; instead they are fragmented or linked by associations in a manner analogous to the stream-of-consciousness technique in literature. The viewer is challenged to put together the pieces and extract the meaning of the work. Many of these new works incorporate movements from outside the range of conventional ballet or modern dance techniques. A spoken text may be delivered by a narrator or by the dancers themselves. Some dances in fact bear close affinities with the concept of the total art work, first promulgated by the court ballet and more recently by the mixed-media productions of the theatre artist Robert Wilson, whose *Einstein on the Beach* (1976) included choreography by Lucinda Childs.

In France, the cradle of ballet, modern dance activity was initially sporadic, although pupils of Duncan, Wigman and others worked there. The 1970s, however, marked the beginning of a lively interchange between French and American dancers and choreographers. The Paris Opéra helped promote this interchange when in 1974 it appointed Carolyn Carlson (b.1943), a former member of Nikolais's company, to head a special ensemble called the Groupe des Recherches Théâtrales de l'Opéra de Paris (GRTOP), composed of dancers from the outside rather than the Opéra's own personnel. Carlson became immensely popular both as a performer and as the choreographer of highly theatrical dances, replete with poetic imagery: *Year of the Horse* (1978), for example, was inspired by the Chinese horoscope figure symbolizing the transcendence of reality.

The Opéra's second venture into modern dance, the Groupe de Recherche Chorégraphique de l'Opéra de Paris (GRCOP), was founded by Jacques Garnier in 1980. It features dancers from the Opéra in works by foreign choreographers such as Karole Armitage, Lucinda Childs, David Gordon and Paul Taylor, as well as French choreographers such as Dominique Bagouet (a former member of Carlson's company), Jean-Christophe Paré, Jean Guizerix and Garnier himself.

Outside Paris, the Centre National de Danse Contemporaine (CNDC) was formed in 1978 in Angers with Nikolais as its first artistic director. He was succeeded in 1981 by Viola Farber (b.1931), a former Cunningham dancer, who established a professional company alongside the school. The CNDC is the only government-subsidized training programme in modern dance in France, although such classes are extremely popular throughout the country; Cunningham technique is an especial favourite.

Most of the modern dance groups now performing in France have been active only since the late 1970s. With the sponsorship of the Ministry of Culture, a number of these groups have been based outside Paris, literally extending the reach of modern dance. Some outstanding examples are the Compagnie Maguy Marin in Créteil; the Compagnie Dominique Bagouet in Montpellier; the Groupe Emile Dubois, led by Jean-Claude Gallotta, in Grenoble; the Théâtre du Silence in La Rochelle (an 'older' group, formed in 1971); and the Compagnie de Danse de l'Esquisse in Paris, founded by Joëlle Bouvier and Regis Obadia.

French modern dance choreography frequently reveals an interest in characterization, connections with literature and cinema (particularly with the surrealists and the absurdists) and the use of speech or dialogue as well as movement. Maguy Marin, a former member of Béjart's company, displays some of these traits in *May B* (1981), which was inspired by the plays of Samuel Beckett. The dancers, dressed in night clothes with grey-powdered faces, do very little dancing in the conventional sense of the word; instead they shuffle along, stamp their feet, push and fondle each other, and mutter or

132 Movements derived from the Chinese exercise system called T'ai Chi Ch'uan add an Eastern flavour to Glen Tetley's Embrace Tiger and Return to Mountain *(1968), danced here by Ballet Rambert members Michael Ho, Mark Wraith, Yair Vardi, Thomas Yang and Sally Owen.*

scream unintelligibly. Costumed as recognizable characters, including Lucky and Pozzo from *Waiting for Godot*, they eat cake at a birthday party. Yet these actions, as limited in their way as those of Beckett's ashcan- or wheelchair-bound characters, capture the emotional atmosphere of Beckett's plays.

Britain has had two major experimental dance groups since the mid-1960s, when Ballet Rambert was reorganized as a contemporary dance ensemble and began to perform works couched in a mixture of classical and modern dance techniques. As in France, American influence was initially strong within both this company and its peer, London Contemporary Dance Theatre. Invited to help build Ballet Rambert's new repertory, the American Glen Tetley created works such as *Embrace Tiger and Return to Mountain* (1968), which took its inspiration from T'ai Chi Ch'uan, a Chinese system of exercise and self-defence. Over the years, London Contemporary Dance Theatre and its affiliated school have gradually dissolved most of their ties with Graham and her company; however, the group continues to perform many works by its first artistic director, Robert Cohan. Another American,

128

Robert North (b.1945), created one of its most popular pieces, *Troy Game*

(1974), a tongue-in-cheek display of male athletic prowess.

Some outstanding British modern dance choreographers include Ballet Rambert's Christopher Bruce (b.1945), who often treats political or social themes. His *Ghost Dances* (1981), dedicated to the people of South America, is a series of solos, duets and ensembles linked by three eerie skull-masked figures whose presence gives the piece an air of a contemporary Dance of Death. Richard Alston (b.1948) has worked with both London Contemporary Dance Theatre and Ballet Rambert (where he is now artistic director) as well as on a freelance basis. In 1972 he formed his own company, Strider, which lasted for three years. *Doublework* (1978), perhaps his best-known work, focuses on three duets performed by three couples. He has also staged a version of *The Rite of Spring* (1981), dedicated to Marie Rambert, who shared with him her memories of working with Nijinsky on the original production. In preparing this ballet he also studied Nijinska's *Les Noces*, which inspired him to use sculpturesque groups and stillness as a contrast to frenetic activity.

Alston has also worked as a guest choreographer for Second Stride, which was named in tribute to his own Strider by its founders, Siobhan Davies and Ian Spink, an Australian. Davies (b.1950), who is also a resident choreographer of London Contemporary Dance Theatre, created the popular *Carnival* (1982) for Second Stride, reinterpreting the beasts in Saint-Saëns' *Carnival of the Animals* in terms of their human equivalents: the tortoises become a pair of senior citizens, the cuckoo a suitor wooing a cold-hearted woman, the aquarium a cocktail-party gathering. The swan's music, usually associated with Pavlova's rendition of *The Dying Swan*, accompanies a man's solo that suggests not only a swan's wings and curving neck but the cellist's bowing of his instrument as he plays the famous theme.

Michael Clark (b.1962), whose dance background includes the Royal Ballet School, the Ballet Rambert and the Cunningham studio, is currently considered the most innovative young choreographer working in Britain today. Recognized as a compelling dancer as well, his works are built on a classical foundation, yet create effects that are boldly iconoclastic. He often uses punk music and costumes, such as the all-over tights with revealing holes worn by the cast of *Do You Me? I Did* (1984). Like Cunningham and the American dancer-choreographer Karole Armitage (see below), with whom he has been associated, he startles audiences by his use of the unexpected. He has been commissioned to choreograph works for a number of ballet companies, among them the Paris Opéra and London Festival Ballet.

Two major new approaches to dance have come from the east and the west respectively. Butoh, from Japan, and Tanztheater, from Germany, both

133 In Grain *(1983) the Butoh-inspired dancers Eiko and Koma evoked a bleak world of hunger and craving.*

began to emerge in the 1960s, but only gained international fame when companies utilizing these approaches visited the U.S. in the 1980s. Butoh is the shortened form of the term *ankotu butoh*, or 'dance of utter darkness'. Its name derives from its prevailing bleakness of vision, which is attributed to the legacy of Hiroshima. It was first developed by Kazuo Ohno (b.1906), his son Yoshito, and Tatsumi Hijikata (d.1986). Butoh rejects both traditional Japanese dance forms such as Noh and Kabuki, and Western modern dance, yet retains a high degree of physical control. Economy of movement characterizes Butoh in general, and time is frequently slowed to a rate that seems excruciating by western standards. But the images Butoh creates are vivid and telling; the dancers' bodies may take on the semblance of non-human creatures or even inanimate objects such as plants or driftwood. Butoh's primary aim is the expression of man's inner life, usually presented from a point of view that is universal rather than individual: intense emotions are represented in a highly stylized manner, and the dancers' faces and bodies are often painted white as though to heighten the anonymity and impersonality of much of human existence.

Life, death and metamorphosis are principal themes of Butoh. In the striking opening of Ushio Amagatsu's *Jomon Sho* [*Homage to Prehistory*] (1982), four members of the Sankai Juku dance company descend to the stage hanging from ropes, head-first, in a metaphor of birth. Ohno has spoken of his awareness of infinite memories of past lives. In his evening-long solo

Admiring La Argentina (1976) he assumes the persona not only of the great Spanish dancer but also of crumbling beauties in bygone fashions and a virile man in a loincloth. The Butoh-influenced dances of Eiko and Koma, two Japanese-born dancers who have worked in the U.S. since 1976, often deal with elemental human needs, expressed through an extreme austerity of movement. In *Grain* (1983) Eiko stuffs rice, the Japanese staple food, into Koma's mouth; in *Thirst* (1985) the couple represents two parched creatures in a desert, searching for the slightest trace of moisture: a drop of perspiration, the hope of milk from a woman's breasts.

Butoh's use of distortion has often been compared to German Expressionism. Ohno's assumption of female dress is in the tradition of the *onnagata* or female impersonator in Kabuki; however, in contrast to the Kabuki actors, the faces of his female characters are clumsily painted as though to deny illusion, and he does not shrink from revealing the ravages of age or suggesting mental abnormality. In *Jomon Sho* the dancers often appear to be mutants or deformities in a world moving post-haste towards destruction. Eiko and Koma set their dances in an ambiguous milieu that could be the beginning of the world, or its end; they often appear to be creatures who have not quite attained humanity, or perhaps have lost it. Butoh is frequently pessimistic in outlook, yet its dark fables can be extraordinarily moving.

Kei Takei, a Japanese dancer who came to the U.S. in 1966, offers a somewhat different worldview. She creates images of a primitive world where man is subservient both to nature and his own rituals, yet she does not share the desolate vision of Butoh; instead she seeks what she calls the sense of 'alive-ing', an unpretentious savouring of existence. Her dance cycle *Light*, begun in 1969, reached its twenty-first part in 1985. Several of its sections depict basic human experiences: labouring in the fields, competing and cooperating with others, supporting the dying, succumbing to one's own death. Takei is little concerned with dance technique, and many of the movements seem to arise naturally from the situation at hand, such as snatching at clothes or collecting the white balloons that represent the harvest. Other movements are extremely simple, almost primitivistic: stamping, clapping hands, clashing stones together. With these she builds a world in which the artifices of the civilized world are stripped away to expose the fundamental nature of human life.

The German movement called Tanztheater (dance theatre) is best known outside Germany through the works of Pina Bausch (b.1940) and her company, the Wuppertaler Tanztheater. Her performers, who are usually dressed in drab contemporary clothes, have the appearance of ordinary men and women rather than the highly trained dancers they actually are. Their activities, some of which seem quite ordinary, acquire a heightened

133

134 The works of Pina Bausch, though highly theatrical in nature, bear little resemblance to traditional ballets. In Auf dem Gebirge Hat Man ein Geschrei Gehört *(1984), the dancers perform on a surface covered by earth, which limits their movements. Bausch eschews technical virtuosity, however, in favour of powerful images that give expression to the pent-up violence and frustration of modern life.*

significance through repetition. A man in *Bluebeard* (1977) obsessively stops and starts a tape recording of Béla Bartók's opera *Bluebeard's Castle*, which gives the piece its name. In *Auf dem Gebirge Hat Man ein Geschrei Gehört [On the Mountains a Cry Was Heard]* (1984), a group of men, perhaps representing bullies on a playground, hotly pursues a man and woman in order to force them to kiss one another.

Bausch's inventions inhabit a world closer to our own than the more stylized creations of Butoh. Although she seldom depicts specific characters, she shows us recognizable human types, such as the long-suffering woman in *Bluebeard* who is repeatedly dragged across the floor on her back by the main male performer, and ultimately appears to suffocate under the multiple layers of clothing in which he dresses her. Men and women carry on a search for love, predatory or pathetic, in the dance hall setting of *Kontakthof* (1978). The battle between the sexes looms large in many of Bausch's works, sometimes expressed with nightmarish violence. Women are almost always the victims, men the aggressors: a group of men symbolically force their unwelcome caresses upon a woman in *Kontakthof*, while in *Bluebeard* a lone attacker works his way systematically down a line of women, who offer no more resistance than a token scream. Yet there can be unexpected moments of serene beauty: in *1980* (1980) a woman gambols, child-like, in the spray of a lawn sprinkler; a woman in *Gebirge*, her face hidden by her long hair, tugs her satiny slip this way and that to form sculpturesque shapes.

Bausch's unconventionality extends to the surfaces upon which her dancers perform. They splash through a pool of water, complete with a fake hippopotamus, in *Arien* [*Arias*] (1979); leaves carpet the stage in *Bluebeard*, earth in *1980* and *Gebirge*. The dancers occasionally speak, sing, scream or laugh: in *1980* they confess their fears to an interrogator. Often they dress in the clothes of the opposite sex. Yet Bausch's works frequently centre upon the failure to communicate or establish contact, and the lack of empathy between individuals and between the sexes. Bitterness, anger and brutality seem to dominate her pieces; unsurprisingly, some viewers react to them with revulsion and hostility.

Yet few would deny that Bausch is generally successful in her primary goal of provoking an emotional response from the audience. A student of Jooss and Tudor, she shares their desire to portray the human condition without shying away from feelings that are unpleasant, disturbing or shameful. Her images are presented in an unsparingly direct manner, without the cushioning of a story or allegory. The viewer is forced to come face-to-face with feelings that most people would prefer to keep hidden.

The works of Meredith Monk (see chapter 10) presaged the return to narrative and symbolism in the U.S. Over the years, her use of symbolism has grown richer and more complex. She now prefers to call her mixed-media works 'operas' and describes herself as a theatre artist rather than a choreographer, for her concerns transcend dance alone. However, movement remains an important element in her works. In *Quarry* (1976), Monk plays the central role of the sick child, who may be a metaphor for Europe in the troubled years before the Second World War. Among the figures who surround her at the beginning of the work are a man and woman dressed in the garments of biblical times. Dictators parade on a red carpet, only to die in succession; performers carry in airplanes on poles; a crowd of chanting marchers stages a rally. A film interlude shows motionless bodies afloat in a pool of water. A black-clad couple, probably destined for a concentration camp, silently drop their valuables to the floor. The weight of history lends power to many of these images: these people seem like more sharply focused versions of the figures in old newsreels or photographs.

135 In Meredith Monk's Quarry *(1976), the woes of war-torn Europe are symbolized by an ailing child (Monk, far left).*

Tharp's first evening-long venture into narrative was *When We Were Very Young* (1980), which incorporated poems from A. A. Milne's collection of the same title. Cast in the experimental form of a 'dansical', it had a script by the playwright Thomas Babe, which told the story of Jane (Tharp), a grown-up woman who dies and goes to Child Heaven. Other members of Tharp's company played Jane's husband, son and daughter. Only Jane had a substantial number of lines to speak, though the dancers sometimes chanted Milne's poems while dancing.

The Catherine Wheel, which Tharp created in the following year, dispenses with dialogue, though the lyrics of David Byrne's accompanying songs sometimes parallel the emotions raised by the action. The scenario is stormy, filled with lust and strife: a husband and wife, and their son and daughter, contend with one another and with their maid, pet and a poet. Their violence is echoed, as in ancient Greek drama, by a chorus which at one point turns against its leader, spinning her about in an orgy of vengefulness. Growing ever larger, a pineapple is passed among the dancers; its golden gleam promises desirable rewards, yet its shape and colloquial meaning hint that it is also an instrument of destruction. A second dominant symbol is the wheel, which appears in the work's title, the stage setting, and the dancers'

cartwheels, simultaneously suggesting the torture of St Catherine of Alexandria, mechanical progress and the cyclical nature of time. The piece ends with the pure-dance 'Golden Section', in which the gold-costumed dancers appear to have been transfigured into beings of a higher order.

Secret Pastures (1984), another recent experiment in narrative dance, was choreographed by Bill T. Jones and Arnie Zane. This excursion into fantasy depicts a mad professor who travels to a desert island with an entourage that includes a 'fabricated man'. All semblance of plot is abandoned, however, as the expedition succumbs to the sensual pleasures of the inhabitants' 'Garden of Radio Delights'. Some critics have discerned in this piece an ironic commentary on the introduction of an innocent (here, the 'fabricated man') to the refinements and vices of civilized society.

With the rise of the antinuclear movement, dancers have once again begun to voice political and social concerns through their art. The group called Dancers for Disarmament, founded in 1981, joined in a major protest march and rally in New York City in 1982. Its members (drawn from across the nation) carried banners and gave simultaneous performances of Remy Charlip's *Flowering Trees* at various outdoor locations in the city. Liz Lerman, a choreographer based in Washington, D.C., often treats political themes in her dances. In one section of *Docudance 1980–1983* (1983), a commentary on the government's current economic and military policies, she conjured up a map of the world through evocative gestures, sometimes hinting at ethnic dance movements, as she named each country in a tender voice. At the close of the piece she starkly announced that missiles were trained upon each of these countries.

American modern dancers have also continued to develop new ways of moving and conveying their ideas in movement form. A large number of today's dancers, more than ever before, have earned college degrees, and many display in their works the intellectual keenness and breadth of vision ideally conferred by advanced education. Karole Armitage, formerly a member of the Cunningham company, used the discipline of academic ballet as a departure point for the high-energy choreography of *Drastic Classicism* (1981), which was accompanied by an earsplitting score by Rhys Chatham and costumed in punk style. $-p = dH/dg$ (1985), later renamed *The Watteau Duets*, combined neon-coloured punk clothing with an assortment of footgear that included pointe shoes, perilously high heels and stilts, each of which enforced different movement choices upon the choreography. The juxtaposition of classicism and punk has been a conspicuous feature of much of her work.

The eclectic movement background of Mark Morris (b.1956) includes Bulgarian folk dance, flamenco, ballet and modern dance; he has danced for choreographers as diverse as Eliot Feld and Laura Dean. He uses a wide variety of music, from the Baroque to pop and ethnic (his solo *O Rangasayee* was danced to an Indian raga), but his dances consistently display both care and ingenuity in their formal structure. These qualities have been welcomed by many viewers, particularly those who believe that the concern for craftsmanship dissipated after the Judson years.

Several choreographers have contrived to incorporate recent advances in modern technology into their works. With the help of split-screen videotape techniques, the cast of Charles Moulton's *Nine-Person Precision Ball-Passing* (1980) was multiplied into a horde seemingly as uncountable as the facets in a fly's eye. Computer-generated images of dancers shared the stage with flesh-and-blood performers in Mel Wong's *Buddha Meets Einstein at the Great Wall* (1985). Maida Withers has created a *Laser Dance* (1985) in collaboration with the laser sculptor Rockne Krebs. Modern technology has served dancers off stage, too: more sophisticated and accessible film and videotape techniques have made it easier to record dances, computers have lightened the tasks of dance administrators and researchers, and a data-processor for notators is reportedly right around the corner.

Experimental fever has also touched the world of ballet, which has adopted some of the music and compositional devices pioneered by choreographers such as Lucinda Childs and Laura Dean. Robbins's *Glass Pieces* (1983) is danced to the minimalist music of Philip Glass. In keeping with the music, his choreography employs repetition, accumulation and the everyday movement of walking, although the company's sleek, highly skilled corps de ballet bears little resemblance to the untrained performers who appeared with the Judson group. Eliot Feld has used the music of Steve Reich in several pieces. He too has adopted the use of repetition, but he adds an extra dimension to his patterns by having his dancers perform on inclined surfaces. In *Aurora I* and *II* (both 1985), a ramp runs the width of the stage, while in *Bent Planes* (1986) a series of ramps form zigzag silhouettes against the backdrop. Like the raked stages of some old European theatres, Feld's ramps alter the dancers' perceptions of gravity and balance. These works are danced in running shoes that better enable the dancers to meet the sheer physical challenges the ramps create.

The experiments of the 1960s have also led to an expansion of the range of serious or artistic dance. This has involved a change in attitude among dancers and choreographers as well as critics, scholars and the general public. Today both performers and spectators have acquired a new interest in dance forms earlier dismissed as commercial or popular. Serious choreographers are again making dances for musical comedies and films, much as they did in the 1930s and 40s. 1985 marked the Broadway premieres of *Singin' in the Rain*, which was directed and choreographed by Tharp, and *Song and Dance*, choreographed by the New York City Ballet's Peter Martins. Highlights from successful musical comedies of the past are presented by Lee Theodore's American Dance Machine, which was founded in 1977 as a living archive of the musical theatre. Its repertory includes excerpts from Holm's *My Fair Lady*, de Mille's *Brigadoon* and *Carousel*, Saddler's *No, No, Nanette*, Fosse's *Sweet Charity* and many others. In addition to performances, the American Dance Machine also offers training in show dancing and is building a library of related source materials. In England, Wayne Sleep (b.1948), a former principal dancer of The Royal Ballet, has founded a company called Dash, which performs a mixed array of ballet, modern, jazz, tap and disco dances. Sleep has also danced in the musicals *Cats* (1981) and *Song and Dance* (1982), the latter choreographed by Anthony Van Laast, who formerly danced with London Contemporary Dance Theatre.

Tap dancing, which lost favour after a heyday in the musical comedies and films of the 1930s and 40s, is now enjoying a revival. Charles 'Honi' Coles is perhaps the most prominent of the black performers who have been rediscovered in the 1970s and 80s. A veteran of the Cotton Club and the Apollo Theatre, renowned showcases for black tap dancers, he has contributed to the renaissance of tap through his performances in musicals such as *Bubbling Brown Sugar* and *My One and Only*, for which he won a Tony award. He also appears with his own group, the Copasetics.

Choreographers are also finding new approaches to tap dancing. Jane Goldberg, whose Changing Times Tap Dance Company helped reawaken interest in Coles, Chuck Green and other older masters of the art, has also invented 'topical tap', which combines tapping and talking. Gail Conrad blends tap with elements of ballet, modern, ballroom and show dancing in narrative works that often involve ensemble tapping, a departure from the traditional solo form. *Travelers: A Tap/Dance Epic* (1978) follows a group of tourists through Latin America as they snap photos, decipher maps and dance to the beat of sambas and rumbas.

John Curry (b.1949), whose aim is to infuse ice skating with the artistic qualities of dancing, first attracted the notice of the dance world when his musicality and fluidity of movement won him a gold medal at the 1976 Winter Olympics. Since 1977 he has presented several ice skating shows with his own company, which he trains in both dance and skating. Several ballet and modern dance choreographers have collaborated with him, sometimes exploiting the similarities between ice skating and dancing, sometimes stretching the skater's vocabulary. Dean's characteristic spinning movements, incorporated into the group work *Burn* (1983), are related to skaters' turns. *After All* (1976), Tharp's challenging solo for Curry, puts together movements in ways new to skating: jumps are performed in rapid succession without long preparatory glides, the body swings more freely in a lunge, a spin is allowed to lose momentum instead of speeding up again. Thanks to Curry's efforts, dance qualities are now emphasized by skaters such as Robin Cousins, Toller Cranston and the duo of Jayne Torvill and Christopher Dean.

Dances of the past, both theatrical and social, have begun to attract new performers and audiences. Mary Skeaping (1902–84), a British dancer and choreographer, was a pioneer of historical dance performance. In the mid-1950s she began to recreate period ballets such as *Cupid Out of His Humour* (1650) in Sweden's Drottningholm Court Theatre. Built in 1766 and abandoned by the 1800s, Drottningholm and its scenery, wardrobe and stage machinery were preserved intact, and today it serves as a living museum of

136, 137 Left, Michael Clark, arguably the most innovative British choreographer of the 1980s, continues to surprise audiences with his unpredictable inventions; right, blending ice skating and theatrical dance, John Curry has worked with choreographers such as Twyla Tharp, Kenneth MacMillan, Peter Martins and Laura Dean.

18th-century performing arts and a testament to the craft and ingenuity of the Baroque era.

In the U.S., historical dance groups are usually led by dancer–historians who reconstruct dances from the notation of the time and research deportment, music, costumes, setting and other elements of dance presentation. Some of these groups specialize in a specific period: the Cambridge Court Dancers, directed by Ingrid Brainard, performs medieval and Renaissance dances such as the pavane, lavolta and galliard. The Court Dance Company of New York, co-directed by Charles Garth and Elizabeth Aldrich, has presented *The Lord's Masque* and *Tirso e Clori*, both dating from the 1610s. Wendy Hilton and Shirley Wynne helped initiate interest in Baroque dance in the U.S. Social and theatrical dances of this period have been reconstructed from Feuillet notation by Janis Pforsich for her company Courante and by Catherine Turocy and Ann Jacoby for the New York Baroque Dance Company. In collaboration with the Concert Royal orchestra, which plays period instruments, the New York Baroque Dance Company has presented full-length revivals of 18th-century operas and opera-ballets, among them Rameau's *Les Indes Galantes*, Gluck's *Orfeo ed Euridice* and Handel's *Ariodante*. Similar work has been done in England by Belinda Quirey, whose reconstructions of Rameau's *Pygmalion* and *Castor et Pollux* were presented by the English Bach Festival in 1976 and 1984 respectively. In Europe, the Baroque period has been explored by Francine Lancelot, leader of the historical dance company Ris et Danceries, who has also used the Baroque dance vocabulary to create *Lulli: Quelques Pas Graves de Baptiste* (1985) for the Paris Opéra Ballet.

Social dances of past centuries have been brought to the stage by Carol Téten's Dance Through Time company, which is based in California. The American Ballroom Theater, co-directed by Pierre Dulaine and Yvonne Marceau, performs 20th-century exhibition ballroom dances such as the waltz, tango, foxtrot and jitterbug. Tango Argentino, an evening-long dance programme, focuses exclusively on the tango, tracing it from its origins in the slums of Buenos Aires to its more refined ballroom versions. The tango is even used as the basis of a mini-drama about a young girl's rise and fall as a prostitute.

Dance notation, criticism and research have begun to attract growing numbers of adherents. Although many dance-related support groups – among them the American Dance Guild, the Congress on Research in Dance, the Dance Critics Association, the Dance Notation Bureau and the Society of Dance History Scholars – were established prior to the 1980s, this decade has seen an astonishing rise in the number of conferences, symposia and other activities available to members of these fields. More interaction now takes place between the disciplines: for example, the Dance Critics Association has sponsored seminars on historical subjects such as the choreography of Goleizovsky. International exchange is promoted by the Dance Committee of the International Theatre Institute, whose first co-presidents were Grigorovich and Joffrey. Some European counterparts of the American organizations include the Society for Dance Research in Britain and the Société Internationale des Enseignants, Chercheurs, Créateurs en Danse, founded by Jean-Claude Serre at the Sorbonne in Paris.

A number of dance notation systems have been devised over the centuries to meet the challenge of preserving choreography. Today the most widely used system is Labanotation, whose basic principles were formulated by Laban but refined by many others. The Dance Notation Bureau in New York City, founded in 1940 with Ann Hutchinson at its head, has played a major role in teaching, disseminating and improving this method. The Bureau also serves as a library, research centre and clearinghouse of information on notation. Benesh Notation was invented in the 1950s by Rudolf and Joan Benesh, who established the Institute of Choreology in 1962. It is used in many ballet companies, particularly in Britain. Noa Eshkol and Abraham Wachman developed Eshkol-Wachman Movement Notation in Israel during the 1950s. It has had many different applications, including animal behaviour, medicine and psychiatry. The practitioners of these three systems met to read papers and exchange views at the First International Congress on Movement Notation, held in Tel Aviv in 1984.

The mounting interest in research and scholarship has incited both dance companies and individuals to become more historically-minded, and many have come to realize that the detritus of the past – financial records, touring schedules, production notes, press releases, scrapbooks and the like – may be valuable source materials for historians of the future. Although scattered collections of such materials can be found in a number of places, the largest and most comprehensive dance archive remains the Dance Collection of the New York Public Library, established in the 1940s under the curatorship of Genevieve Oswald. The collection includes not only printed materials but notation scores, photographs, artworks, audiotapes, films, videotapes and other objects – an unparalleled treasury of resources on dance. Among its holdings are issues of the numerous dance periodicals that are published today in many different countries, enabling a free flow of information on current dance activities all over the world.

If the sedentary pursuit of dance scholarship has gained popularity, so has a more active type of dance phenomenon that has often been likened to sports: the international ballet competition. The first such competition was held in Varna, Bulgaria, in 1964, where an international array of dancers gathered to compete for medals, much in the manner of the Olympics. Since then, similar competitions have been held, sometimes on a regular basis, in the cities of Moscow, Osaka, Helsinki, New York, Paris and Jackson, Mississippi. The competitors perform before panels of established dancers and choreographers: Ulanova, Alonso, Grigorovich and Joffrey have all served on such juries. Prizes may include medals, diplomas and money; the Prix de Lausanne, a competition for young dance students, offers scholarships to ballet academies. Though some dancers feel that these competitions place unnecessary strains on the entrants, others believe that participation in competitions can provide welcome publicity that will boost their careers.

The image of the dancer as athlete, implicit in the demanding choreography of many dance works and more openly stated by the ballet competitions, has come closer to reality as more people incorporate some form of dance into their physical fitness regimens. Aerobic dancing, designed to improve cardiovascular functioning, is today practised by many men and women for the combined purposes of good health and enjoyment. Others study jazz, tap, ballet, modern and ethnic dance as a form of exercise, and non-professional dance classes have burgeoned thanks to the fitness boom. As a side-effect of this boom, dancers' practice clothing has become fashionable: for instance, knitted legwarmers, which dancers invented to keep their muscles warm during rehearsals, may now be purchased in colours that coordinate with one's leotard, tights and sweatband, and are worn as a chic accessory even in overheated exercise studios.

Isadora Duncan once declared, in a paraphrase of Walt Whitman, 'I see America dancing.' In a sense her prophecy has come true not only for the U.S. but for many other parts of the world. Dance may no longer be a repository of magical power, as it was in preliterate cultures, nor does it wield the same political clout of the court ballet, but it has become a fulfilling part of many people's lives. Ballet, once the pastime of kings, is now watched and enjoyed by all segments of society, as are the many other forms of theatrical dance. Moreover, growing numbers of people are beginning to participate actively in various dance forms, rather than regarding dance as a spectator sport. Isadora, one suspects, would have approved.

Select Bibliography

Two reference books that may be recommended despite a few inaccuracies and some outdated articles are *The Dance Encyclopedia*, compiled and edited by Anatole Chujoy and P.W. Manchester (revised and enlarged edition, New York, Simon and Schuster, 1967), and Horst Koegler's *The Concise Oxford Dictionary of Ballet* (second edition, London, Oxford University Press, 1982), which offers useful bibliographic references for many entries.

Selections from technical and theoretical writings from the 16th to the 20th centuries are reprinted in *Dance as a Theatre Art: Source Readings in Dance History from 1581 to the Present*, edited with a commentary by Selma Jeanne Cohen and an extensive bibliography (New York, Harper & Row, 1974). Lincoln Kirstein's *Movement & Metaphor* (New York, Praeger, 1970), which has been reissued as a Dover paperback under the title *Four Centuries of Ballet*, provides a scholarly analysis of fifty major ballets from the French court ballet on.

A number of useful books are devoted to the dance of a single country. Marcia B. Siegel's *The Shapes of Change: Images of American Dance* (Boston, Houghton Mifflin, 1979) analyses several landmarks of American ballet and modern dance. Robert Coe's *Dance in America* (New York, Dutton, 1985) includes informative short histories of several major ballet and modern dance companies. The development of five major British companies is chronicled in *Twentieth Century Dance in Britain*, edited by Joan W. White (London, Dance Books, 1985). Ivor Guest's *Le Ballet de l'Opéra de Paris: Trois siècles d'histoire et de tradition*, translated by Paul Alexandre (Paris, Théâtre National de l'Opéra, 1976), focuses on a single but highly influential company, the Paris Opéra Ballet. Russian ballet from 1770 to 1965 is covered by Natalia Roslavleva's *Era of the Russian Ballet* (London, Gollancz, 1966).

Readers interested in the choreographic process may consult *Making a Ballet* by Clement Crisp and Mary Clarke (New York, Macmillan, 1975). The historical relationships of music and dance are explored in Baird Hastings's *Choreographer and Composer* (Boston, Twayne, 1983). Clarke and Crisp have also collaborated on *Design for Ballet* (New York, Hawthorne Books, 1978), a lavishly illustrated history of scenery and costume design. *Designing for the Dancer* (London, Elron Press, 1981) includes scholarly essays on dance costumes by Roy Strong, Ivor Guest and Richard Buckle.

Plot synopses of ballets are always popular, and new books of this type are constantly published to reflect the ever-changing repertory. A perennially useful source for the dance historian is Cyril W. Beaumont's *Complete Book of Ballets* (London, Putnam, 1937) which includes the librettos of many past ballets. Beaumont also published several supplements to this book. A more up-to-date selection is found in George Balanchine and Francis Mason's *Balanchine's Complete Stories of the Great Ballets* (revised and enlarged edition, Garden City, New York, Doubleday, 1977).

For those intrigued by the possibilities of dance notation, Ann Hutchinson Guest's *Dance Notation: The Process of Recording Movement on Paper* (Brooklyn, New York, Dance Horizons, 1984) discusses the theory and history of the subject.

The beginnings of ballet are chronicled in Roy Strong's colourfully illustrated *Splendour at Court: Renaissance Spectacle and Illusion* (London, Weidenfeld and Nicolson, 1972), in Margaret M. McGowan's *L'Art du ballet de cour en France 1581–1643* (Paris, Editions du Centre National de la Recherche Scientifique, 1963), and in Marie-Françoise Christout's *Le Ballet de cour de Louis XIV 1643–1672* (Paris, Editions A. et J. Picard, 1967). In *Dance of Court & Theater: The French Noble Style 1690–1725* (Princeton, New Jersey, Princeton Book Co., 1981), Wendy Hilton prefaces her technical analyses of the dances with a fascinating general discussion of 18th-century court life, dancing masters and deportment. Richard Ralph's *The Life and Works of John Weaver* (New York, Dance Horizons, 1985) is a biography supported by reprints of Weaver's treatises and librettos. Jean Georges Noverre's *Letters on Dancing and Ballets*, translated by Cyril W. Beaumont (London, Beaumont, 1930), may be read in conjunction with Deryck Lynham's biography *The Chevalier Noverre: Father of Modern Ballet* (London, Sylvan Press, 1950) for a vivid picture of the ballet of the time as well as Noverre's life and ideas. Bridging the 18th and 19th centuries is Marian Hannah Winter's *The Pre-Romantic Ballet* (London, Pitman, 1974), which covers popular entertainment as well as ballet. Mary Grace Swift's *A Loftier Flight: The Life and Accomplishments of Charles-Louis Didelot, Balletmaster* (Middletown, Conn., Wesleyan University Press/London, Pitman, 1974) also provides a detailed description of this transitional period.

The history of the Romantic ballet is well documented by Ivor Guest's many fine studies, among them *The Romantic Ballet in Paris* (second, revised edition, London, Dance Books, 1980), *The Romantic Ballet in England* (London, Phoenix House, 1954), *The Ballet of the Second Empire* (London, A. & C. Black, 1953, 1955) and the monumental biography *Jules Perrot: Master of the Romantic Ballet* (New York, Dance Horizons, 1984). August Bournonville tells his own story in *My Theatre Life*, translated and annotated by Patricia N. McAndrew (Middletown, Conn., Wesleyan University Press, 1979). The memoirs of Marius Petipa, translated by Helen Whittaker and edited by Lillian Moore, have been published as *Russian Ballet Master* (London, A. & C. Black, 1958). The musicologist Roland John Wiley focuses on three Petipa-Ivanov masterworks in *Tchaikovsky's Ballets: Swan Lake, The Sleeping Beauty, The Nutcracker* (Oxford, Clarendon Press/New York, Oxford University Press, 1985). 19th-century American ballet is represented by Mary Grace Swift's *Belles and Beaux on Their Toes: Dancing Stars in Young America* (Washington, D.C., University Press of America, 1980).

Diaghilev's achievements have inspired many writings. Richard Buckle's *Diaghilev* (New York, Atheneum, 1979) is considered the definitive biography of the great impresario. An insider's view of the Ballets Russes is supplied by its régisseur Serge Grigoriev in *The Diaghilev Ballet* (London, Constable, 1953), while Nesta Macdonald examines critical responses in *Diaghilev Observed by Critics in England & the United States 1911–1929* (New York, Dance Horizons/London, Dance Books, 1975). A highly recommended interdisciplinary analysis is Martin Battersby's essay on the company's influence on fashion and interior design, published in Charles Spencer's *The World of Serge Diaghilev* (Harmondsworth, Middlesex, Penguin, 1974).

Several members of Diaghilev's company have written autobiographies. Tamara Karsavina's *Theatre Street* (New York, Dutton, 1931), a classic of dance literature, recounts the ballerina's experiences with wit and grace. Michel Fokine's *Fokine: Memoirs of a Ballet Master* (Boston, Little, Brown, 1961) should be supplemented by Cyril W. Beaumont's *Michel Fokine and His Ballets* (London, Beaumont, 1935). Two contrasting points of view are found in *Nijinsky* by the dancer's wife Romola Nijinsky (New York, Simon and Schuster, 1935) and the more scholarly *Nijinsky* by Richard Buckle (New York, Simon and Schuster, 1972). Bronislava Nijinska details her brother's early career as well as her own in *Early Memoirs*, translated and edited by Irina Nijinska and Jean Rawlinson (New York, Holt, Rinehart and Winston, 1981). Léonide Massine's *My Life in Ballet* (New York, St Martin's Press, 1968) and Serge Lifar's *Ma Vie*, translated into English by James Holman Mason

(London, Hutchinson, 1970), depict their beginnings with Diaghilev as well as their later work.

The literature on Diaghilev's counterparts includes *Les Ballets Suédois dans l'art contemporain* (Paris, Editions du Trianon, 1931), which contains contributions by Cocteau, Milhaud, Pirandello, Picabia and others. Keith Money's definitive biography *Anna Pavlova: Her Life and Art* (New York, Knopf, 1982) is a treasurehouse of facts and photographs. The histories of the two principal heirs of the Ballets Russes are described in Jack Anderson's *The One and Only: The Ballet Russe de Monte Carlo* (New York, Dance Horizons, 1981) and Kathrine Sorley Walker's *De Basil's Ballets Russes* (London, Hutchinson, 1982). Sono Osato's autobiography *Distant Dances* (New York, Knopf, 1980) gives a fascinating view of a dancer's life in those days, as do Agnes de Mille's books *Dance to the Piper* and *And Promenade Home* (Boston, Little, Brown, 1952 and 1958).

Two giants of British ballet have also written autobiographies: Marie Rambert's *Quicksilver* (London, Macmillan, 1972) and Ninette de Valois's *Come Dance With Me* (London, Hamish Hamilton, 1957). Alexander Bland's *The Royal Ballet: The First Fifty Years* (Garden City, New York, Doubleday, 1981) is a detailed history of the company. A great British choreographer is the focus of David Vaughan's *Frederick Ashton and His Ballets* (New York, Knopf, 1977).

Since the death of George Balanchine in 1983, books about him have proliferated. Bernard Taper's *Balanchine: A Biography* (New York, Times Books, 1984) is a revised and updated version of a book first published in 1963. Balanchine's longtime associate, Lincoln Kirstein, has published his own account of their work in *Thirty Years: Lincoln Kirstein's The New York City Ballet* (New York, Knopf, 1978). The repertories of the various Balanchine-Kirstein companies, including ballets by other choreographers, are examined in Nancy Reynolds's *Repertory in Review* (New York, Dial, 1977). Another great American company is chronicled in text and pictures in Charles Payne's *American Ballet Theatre* (New York, Knopf, 1978).

Despite its title, Alexander Demidov's *The Russian Ballet: Past and Present*, translated by Guy Daniels (Garden City, New York, Doubleday, 1977) is mainly devoted to the Bolshoi Ballet in the 20th century; however, it also glances at the Kirov and lesser known Russian companies. Pierre Michaut's *Le Ballet contemporain 1929–1950* (Paris, Plon, 1950) examines the work of Roland Petit and other French choreographers of the time.

The modern dance has inspired several historical surveys. Margaret Lloyd's *The Borzoi Book of Modern*

Dance (New York, Knopf, 1949) offers vivid first-hand descriptions of dancers and works. In *Where She Danced* (New York, Knopf, 1979), Elizabeth Kendall analyses the theatrical and educational milieu of American modern dance. The *Complete Guide to Modern Dance* (New York, Doubleday, 1976), by Don McDonagh, takes an encyclopaedic approach, with brief biographies and chronologies of each choreographer.

Studies focusing on individual dancers include Margaret Haile Harris's *Loie Fuller: Magician of Light*, the catalogue of an exhibition held at the Virginia Museum in Richmond, Virginia, in 1979; and Sally R. Sommer's article 'Loie Fuller', in *Drama Review* 19 (1975), 53–67. Isadora Duncan discusses her own life and ideas in *My Life* (New York, Boni and Liveright, 1927) and the posthumous *The Art of the Dance*, edited by Sheldon Chaney (New York, Theatre Arts, 1928). *Ruth St. Denis: An Unfinished Life* (New York/London, Harper, 1939) and Ted Shawn's *One Thousand and One Night Stands* (Garden City, New York, Doubleday, 1960), written in collaboration with Gray Poole, are autobiographies which should be supplemented by Suzanne Shelton's *Divine Dancer: A Biography of Ruth St. Denis* (Garden City, New York, Doubleday, 1981) and Walter Terry's *Ted Shawn: Father of American Dance* (New York, Dial, 1976). A former Denishawn dancer, Jane Sherman, sums up the era in *Denishawn: The Enduring Influence* (Boston, Twayne, 1983).

German modern dance is represented by Rudolf Laban's autobiography *A Life for Dance*, translated and annotated by Lisa Ullmann (New York, Theatre Arts Books, 1975), and two anthologies of the compelling writings of Mary Wigman, *The Language of Dance*, translated by Walter Sorell (Middletown, Conn., Wesleyan University Press, 1966) and *The Mary Wigman Book: Her Writings*, translated and edited by Sorell (Middletown, Conn., Wesleyan University Press, 1975).

Ernestine Stodelle's *Deep Song: The Dance Story of Martha Graham* (New York, Schirmer/London, Collier Macmillan, 1984) and *Doris Humphrey: An Artist First* (Middletown, Conn., Wesleyan University Press, 1972), an autobiography edited and completed by Selma Jeanne Cohen, detail the lives of two giants of American modern dance. Larry Warren's *Lester Horton, Modern Dance Pioneer* (New York, Dekker, 1977) is a biography of the West Coast choreographer. The work of Alwin Nikolais is the subject of 'Nik, a Documentary', edited by Marcia B. Siegel, in *Dance Perspectives* 48 (1971). Merce Cunningham's *Changes: Notes on Choreography* (New York, Something Else Press, 1968) is as puckishly iconoclastic as his choreography; his ideas are more conventionally expressed in conversations with Jacqueline Lesschaeve in *The Dancer and the Dance* (New York/London, Marion Boyars, 1985). Historical surveys, essays, and interviews with avant-garde choreographers such as Trisha Brown, Lucinda Childs and Laura Dean are included in the profusely illustrated *Contemporary Dance*, edited by Anne Livet (New York, Abbeville Press, 1978). Sally Banes provides a lucid analysis of an often bewildering genre in *Terpsichore in Sneakers: Post-Modern Dance* (Boston, Houghton Mifflin, 1980). Interviews with contemporary choreographers, together with chronologies of their works, may be found in Connie Kreemer's *Further Steps: Fifteen Choreographers on Modern Dance* (New York, Harper and Row, 1987).

Dance in films and musicals has recently begun to attract the attention of scholars. Arlene Croce's *The Fred Astaire & Ginger Rogers Book* (New York, 1972) is a readable and informative guide to the Astaire and Rogers films; John Mueller's *Astaire Dancing: The Musical Films* (New York, Knopf, 1985) broadens the scope to include Astaire's other partners. Jerome Delamater's scholarly study *Dance in the Hollywood Musical* (Ann Arbor, Michigan, UMI Research Press, 1981) may be read in conjunction with Tony Thomas's lavishly illustrated *That's Dancing* (New York, Abrams, 1984).

Reviews in newspapers and magazines are a valuable source of information on dance both past and present. Reviews from the 1930s onward may be found in Edwin Denby's *Dance Writings*, edited by Robert Cornfield and William MacKay (New York, Knopf, 1986). Richard Buckle wittily covers the dance scene in Britain since the 1940s in *Buckle at the Ballet* (New York, Atheneum, 1980). Some recent collections by contemporary American critics are Arlene Croce's *Going to the Dance* (New York, Knopf, 1982), Deborah Jowitt's *The Dance in Mind: Profiles and Reviews 1976–1983* (Boston, David R. Godine, 1985) and Marcia B. Siegel's *Watching the Dance Go By* (Boston, Houghton Mifflin, 1977).

The journal *Attitudes and Arabesques*, published in Palo Alto, California, focuses on updating dance literature (both books and articles) and is a valuable aid in building a bibliography. Some other periodicals currently published in the United States are *Dancemagazine*, *Dance Chronicle*, *Dance Research Journal*, *Ballet Review* and *Attitude*. British periodicals include the venerable *Dancing Times*, *Dance and Dancers* and *New Dance*. *Danse*, *Pour la danse*, *Danser: Voir et vivre la danse* and *Les Saisons de la danse* are published in France, while Germany offers *Ballett-Journal/Das Tanzarchiv* and the bilingual (German and English) *Ballett-International*, and in the USSR there is *Sovietskii Balet*.

Acknowledgments for Photographs

All Sport, London/Tony Duffy 137; Bauhaus-Archiv, Museum für Gestaltung, Berlin 76; Béjart's Ballet of the Twentieth Century, Brussels/Claire Falcy 120; Trisha Brown Company, New York/Carol Goodden 117; Chimera Foundation for Dance, New York/David Berlin 109; Courtauld Institute of Art, London 9; Anthony Crickmay 132; Cullberg Ballet Company/The Swedish National Theatre Centre, Stockholm. L. Leslie-Spinks 127; Zoe Dominic 121, 129; Malcolm Dunbar 92; Arnold Eagle 80; Johann Elbers 108, 112; English Bach Festival, Chris Davies/Network 29; Lois Greenfield 115, 133, 135; Richard Haughton 136; International Museum of Photography at George Eastman House, Rochester, N.Y. 58; Laban Centre for Movement and Dance, at University of London Goldsmiths' College, New Cross, London SE14 6NW 63, 65; Raymond Mander and Joe Mitchenson Theatre Collection, London 66; Jack Mitchell 106; Barbara Morgan 79, 82; Jakob Mydtskov 32; National Film Archive, London 104; Dance Collection, The New York Public Library at Lincoln Center, Astor, Lenox and Tilden Foundations 17, 18, 43, 49, 57, 59, 60, 61, 62, 78, 84, 85, 87, 89, 90, 97, 99, 100, 101, 102, 103, 107; Novosti Press Agency, London (Collection of Natalia Roslavleva) 40, 46, 77 (photo A. Saikov); Bertram Park 91; By courtesy of the Rank Organisation, London 125; Royal Opera House, London 44, 93, 94, 126 (Frederika Davis); Society for Cultural Relations with the USSR, London 105; Walter Strate/Dance Collection, The New York Public Library at Lincoln Center, Astor, Lenox and Tilden Foundations 83; L. Sully-Jaulmes 47; Martha Swope 1, 81, 98, 110, 119, 122, 123, 130; Twyla Tharp Foundation, New York/Tom Berthiaume 114; Theatre Museum, London/J.W. Debenham 95; The Times Newspapers Ltd, London 73; Jack Vartoogian 111; Kurt Weill Foundation, London 96; Reg Wilson 45, 50, 113, 116, 118, 124, 128; Wuppertal Dance Theatre/Ulli Weiss 131, 134.

Additional Sources of Illustrations

2 Private Collection; 3 Engraving by Jacques Patin, from Balthazar de Beaujoyeulx, *Le Ballet Comique de la Royne*, Paris, 1582; 4 Drawing by Antoine Caron, 1573, courtesy of the Harvard University Art Museums (Fogg Art Museum), gift Winslow Ames; 5 Wood engraving attributed to Daniel Rabel from the libretto of *Le Ballet de la Délivrance de Renaud*, 1617, Bibliothèque Nationale, Paris; 6 Drawing, *c.* 1629, Bibliothèque Nationale, Paris; 7 Anonymous French drawing, *c.* 1660, Victoria and Albert Museum, London; 9, 10 Drawings by Inigo Jones, 1631, Devonshire Collection. Reproduced by permission of the Trustees of the Chatsworth Settlement; 11 Engraving by Daniel Marot, Bibliothèque Nationale, Paris; 12 Bibliothèque Nationale, Paris; 13 From Raoul Auger Feuillet, *Choréographie*, 1701; 14 Victoria and Albert Museum, London; 15 Drawing by Henri Bonnart, Bibliothèque Nationale, Paris; 16 Painting by Nicolas Lancret, *c.* 1740, National Gallery of Art, Washington, Mellon Collection 1937; 17 Engraving by Pouquet after Nicolas Lancret, 1730, The New York Public Library; 19 Engraving by Bernardo Bellotto, 1758; 20 Devonshire Collection, Chatsworth, reproduced by permission of the Trustees of the Chatsworth Settlement; 21 Watercolour by Louis René Boquet, Bibliothèque Nationale, Paris; 22 Pastel by Jean-Baptiste Perroneau, 1764, Bibliothèque Nationale, Paris; 23 Etching and aquatint by Francesco Bartolozzi, possibly after Nathaniel Dance, 1781, Theatre Museum, London; 24 Theatre Museum, London; 25, 26 Bibliothèque Nationale, Paris; 27 Etching and engraving by Francesco Bartolozzi after Nathaniel Dance, 1781, Theatre Museum, London; 28 Drawing by Johann Gottfried Schadow, 1797, from Hans Mackowsky, *Schadows Graphik*, Berlin, 1936. Institut für Musikwissenschaft der Universität Salzburg, Derra de Moroda Dance Archives; 30, 31 Coloured lithographs after Alfred Edward Chalon, *c.* 1846 and 1845, Victoria and Albert Museum, London; 33 Etching by James Gillray, 1796, Victoria and Albert Museum, London; 34 Bibliothèque Nationale, Paris. 35 Anonymous print after Achille Deveria, Victoria and Albert Museum, London; 36 Lithograph after the drawing by Jules Challamel, 1843, Victoria and Albert Museum, London; 37 Coloured lithograph after J. Bouvier, *c.* 1846, Victoria and Albert Museum, London; 38 Lithograph by John Brandard, Victoria and Albert Museum, London; 39 Lithograph, 19th century, courtesy of the Teatermuseet, Copenhagen; 41 Victoria and Albert Museum, London; 42 Cover of *Il Teatro Illustrato*, March 1881, Museo Teatrale alla Scala, Milan; 47 Watercolour by Léon Bakst, 1909, Musée des Arts Décoratifs, Paris; 48 Wadsworth Atheneum, Hartford, The Serge Lifar Collection, Ella Gallup Sumner and Mary Catlin Sumner Collection; 51 Musée Rodin, Paris; 53 Private Collection, Paris; 54 The Brooklyn Museum, 39.25; 55, 56, 67 Victoria and Albert Museum, London; 68 Musée National d'Art Moderne, Paris; 69, 70 Bibliothèque Nationale, Paris; 71 Fitzwilliam Museum, Cambridge; 72, 74 Victoria and Albert Museum, London; 75 Dansmuseet, Stockholm; 86 Bibliothèque Nationale, Paris.

Index